JER(

in your pocket

Travel Publications

MAIN CONTRIBUTOR: PAUL MURPHY

PHOTOGRAPH CREDITS
All photos supplied by The Travel Library:
John R Jones back cover, 5, 22, 33, 46, 59;
R Richardson 35, 76; David Silverman front cover,
title page, 6, 8, 11, 14, 17, 19, 21, 25, 26, 27, 28, 29, 31,
32, 36, 37, 38, 39, 40, 41, 42, 44, 45, 47, 48, 49, 50, 51,
52, 53, 54, 56, 57, 60, 61, 62, 63, 64(t, b), 66, 67, 68,
69, 70, 71, 72, 74, 75, 78, 81, 82, 83, 84, 87, 89, 90, 92,
95, 96, 97, 98, 102, 105, 106, 107, 109, 111, 113, 118,
120, 123, 125.

front cover: Western Wall, with the Dome of the Rock beyond;
back cover: Mount of Olives and the Garden of Gethsemane;
title page: wall plaque, Jaffa Gate.

MANUFACTURE FRANÇAISE DES PNEUMATIQUES MICHELIN

Place des Carmes-Déchaux – 63000 Clermont-Ferrand (France)

© Michelin et Cie. Propriétaires-Éditeurs 2001

Dépôt légal Jan 01 – ISBN 2-06-000195-1 – ISSN 1272-1689

No part of this publication may be reproduced in any form

without the prior permission of the publisher.

Printed in Spain 01-01

MICHELIN TRAVEL PUBLICATIONS
Michelin Tyre plc
The Edward Hyde Building
38 Clarendon Road
WATFORD Herts WD1 1SX - UK
☎ (01923) 415000
www.michelin-travel.com

MICHELIN TRAVEL PUBLICATIONS
Michelin North America
One Parkway South
GREENVILLE, SC 29615
☎ 1-800 423-0485
www.michelin-travel.com

CONTENTS

INTRODUCTION

Jerusalem is more, much more, than just a mere city. Its very name evokes legends and history: David, Solomon, Jesus, Mohammed, have all been here and all have left their mark. Millions of pilgrims venerate the city annually, yet you don't have to be a believer to feel its sense of awe.

Jerusalem (Yerushalayim) has had many names: City of David, after the boy king who slew Goliath and captured the city for the Israelites; the Golden City, after its magnificent golden-topped Dome of the Rock; the City of Peace, a bitter misnomer for a place where so much blood has been shed and which is still the most disputed city on earth. The Arabs call it simply *Al Quds,* meaning The Holy Place, which no one can deny.

Once it was the centre of the world, both geographically (when the known world was a much smaller place) and spiritually. And it is said that on the Day of Judgement it will be the centre again, when the Messiah strides across the Mount of Olives and leads the resurrected souls into the Old City through the Golden Gate.

With such a reputation then, can today's city really deliver to the modern traveller all that is asked of it? Ironically it may be a better place for the merely curious than for the seriously devoted. It is said that Mark Twain advised the early Zionists to put up signs at all the holy places saying, 'Do not trouble to stop here, it isn't genuine.' In fact the cold, scientific, empirical truth is that Twain was right. Not a single site can be proved as being definitely linked to Jesus, or indeed any other biblical character. In any other city this would be a fatal flaw – Jerusalem, however, is a city of unshakeable belief, where faith overshadows fact and historical proof is a mere detail.

Jerusalem is (and always has been) a far cry from the principles set out on the Ten Commandments tablets that may still lie buried beneath Temple Mount today: commercialised, brusque, intolerant, even duplicitous. Yet, despite all its failings, it retains its mystique and remains one of the world's few truly inspiring cities. It's unlikely you will be disappointed.

Looking across the Muslim Quarter to the Dome of the Rock, with the Mount of Olives beyond.

BACKGROUND

GEOGRAPHY

Jerusalem is not only the spiritual heart of
Israel but its geographic navel too, set
almost halfway between Lebanon 220km
(140 miles) to the north and Eilat 250km
(160 miles) to the south, some 60km
(38 miles) due east of Tel Aviv and 40km
(24 miles) west of the River Jordan which
marks the border with Jordan.

As you will appreciate when approaching

from Tel Aviv (Yafo), the city occupies a dramatic high point on the Judean Hills, over 800m (2 550ft) above sea-level. Here the fertile coastal lands of the west dry up, and beyond, to the south and east of Jerusalem lie the Judean Desert and the Dead Sea. Due north is the biblical wilderness of Samaria, most of which now comes under Palestinian administration and is part of the disputed territory known as the West Bank.

Aerial view of Jerusalem.

Modern Greater Jerusalem has become a sprawl, extending ever outwards in all directions. Visitors, however, can largely disregard this. The Jerusalem they have come to see is a relatively compact place, with the vast majority of its holy sites and attractions either inside the Old City or within a stone's throw of its walls.

HISTORY

Jebusites to Israelites

The first settlements in this region of the Holy Land date as far back as 7000 BC to Jericho (40km/24 miles east of Jerusalem), which in fact is the world's oldest-known walled town. Jerusalem itself has evidence of settlement dating back to 4000 BC, though the foundation of the first city is generally credited to the tribe known as the **Jebusites**, sometime during the second millennium BC. Around 1200 BC, Moses and Joshua led the exodus of the **Israelite** tribe from Egypt back to the Promised Land of Israel, famously bringing down the walls of Jericho en route. When they got to Jerusalem, however, the city walls were made of sterner stuff and the Israelites had to wait another 200 years before **David** finally conquered Jerusalem for them in around 1000 BC.

The First Temple Period

David fortified the city, made it the capital of his kingdom and installed the **Ark of the Covenant**, which had been brought by the Israelites from Egypt and which contained the sacred tablets of the Ten Commandments. The Ark served both as a symbol of sanctity of the city and also united the 12 disparate Israeli tribes. Around 965 BC David died and was succeeded by his son **Solomon**, famed for his wisdom, for his copper mines (near modern-day Eilat) and

Remains of the steps leading up to the Temple can still be seen.

as builder of the **First Temple** c 950 BC. The latter was a magnificent structure, at the heart of which sat the Ark of the Covenant. Under Solomon Jerusalem flourished, with a grand royal palace, mansions for the king's wives, and defensive towers commensurate with a city that was the capital of a powerful empire.

This glorious empire crumbled when Solomon died, around 928 BC, and the Israelites split in two. Two of the tribes chose to stay in Jerusalem (the **House, or Kingdom, of Judah**), while the rest moved north to Samaria to form the **House of Israel**. In 721 BC the **Assyrians** invaded, conquered the land and dispersed the House of Israel, who subsequently became known as the Ten Lost Tribes. Jerusalem reinforced its walls and, with the aid of a hidden water tunnel, managed to withstand the siege. But in 586 BC disaster overtook this House too when the **Babylonians** (who had replaced the Assyrians as the region's dominant power) razed the city, including Solomon's Temple. Its inhabitants were sent into exile and for the next 50 years or so were left to weep by the rivers of Babylon, while what was left of Jerusalem lay empty.

The Second Temple Period

Help was at hand from Cyrus of Persia, who defeated the Babylonians in 539 BC, and allowed the House of Judah (by now, termed Jews) to return home, led by the prophets **Haggai** and **Zechariah**. A **Second Temple**, plainer than the First, was completed around 515 BC, on the same site as the original. Jerusalem was now a province of the **Persian Empire** and remained so until it was conquered by **Alexander the Great**, in

332 BC. Following his death soon after, it passed to the Egyptian **Ptolemy** dynasty, but in 198 BC they were overthrown by the Syrian **Seleucids** who brought their Greek culture to the city, and to the horror of traditional Jews, outlawed Judaism, re-dedicated the Temple to Zeus and, worst sacrilege of all, sacrificed a pig upon its altars. This sparked off a revolt, led by the **Maccabee** (or Hasmonean) brothers, which developed into a full-scale fight for independence. The Maccabees were victorious, and the Hasmonean dynasty ruled Jerusalem and the surrounding lands for the next 115 years, until it fell to the Romans.

The Romans
The Romans treated Jerusalem as a vassal state with limited authority, its own king, and called it Judea. **Herod the Great**, notorious for the massacre of the innocents (according to the Bible), was also the first real city architect, completely rebuilding the Temple, among many other projects. The people, however, hated Herod for taxing and enslaving them in order to accomplish his works. He died in 4 BC, after which the Romans installed procurators (governors) to rule Jerusalem, the most famous being **Pontius Pilate**.

Jesus was born, according to Matthew, during the time of King Herod, which would have to be before 4 BC. Also according to Matthew, he was a direct descendant of Abraham and David and therefore a legitimate claimant to the Jewish throne. Despite his subsequent universal influence, he had little discernible immediate effect on the city.

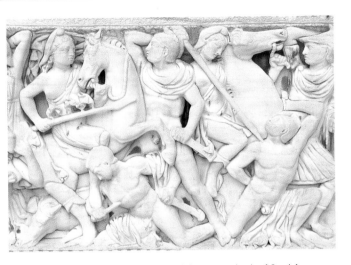

Detail from an early 3C AD Roman tomb, Rockefeller Museum.

The first of the two principal Jewish Revolts occurred in AD 66, ignited by the murder of Jewish citizens and the pillage of the Temple by the procurator. This **First Revolt**, as it became known, drove the Romans out of the city, and prompted rebellions all over Palestine and Syria which kept the Roman legions busy for four years. However in AD 70, during the Passover, when the city was extraordinarily full, the Romans finally arrived at the city gates. After a dreadful siege, during which thousands died of famine alone, the Romans at last entered the city, destroyed the Second Temple, slaughtered many of the city's survivors and took the rest into captivity.

Many of the remaining Jews were exiled or enslaved, but enough remained to stage a **Second Revolt** in AD 132, led by Simon Bar Kochba. The fighting went on for four years and reprisals were savage. Whole villages were destroyed, and thousands were sold into slavery, taken to Rome and other parts of the Roman Empire. Many others fled the country as refugees. This large-scale dispersion of the Jewish people which followed the First and Second Revolts became known as the **Diaspora**.

The Romans, under the **Emperor Hadrian**, rebuilt Jerusalem as Aelia Capitolina, its format corresponding approximately to the Old City as we see it today. Those Jews that were left in Palestine (the Roman name for the province) were banned from the city.

Christianity, a burgeoning underground movement, was officially recognised in 313 by the **Emperor Constantine**. His mother, **Helena**, made a pilgrimage to the city to identify places associated with Jesus, and discovered the True Cross in a cave next to the site of the Holy Sepulchre. Constantine ordered a church to be erected here and Helena built shrines on more places where Christ had been, including the Church of the Holy Sepulchre and the Church of the Nativity (in Bethlehem).

During the Byzantine period, lasting for the next two centuries, Jerusalem recovered and began to flourish again. Disaster overtook it once more in 614, when the Persian Sassanian Empire destroyed the city and, abetted by Samaritans and Jews (who had been oppressed under Byzantine rule), massacred around 33 000 of the city's Christian inhabitants and destroyed its monuments. In 629 Byzantine Emperor Heraclius repelled the Persians and reconquered Jerusalem, and there followed a spate of Jew-killing in retribution for the Christians killed by the Persians and Jews.

Muslims and Crusaders

Jerusalem was not to remain a Christian city for long, however. In 638 as the Arab armies swept across the East, Jerusalem capitulated without bloodshed. Islam also regarded Jerusalem as 'The Holy Place', *Al Quds*, from where **Mohammed** ascended on his Night Journey on a winged horse, through the seven heavens to paradise, where he met God himself (as told in the *Koran*). In 691, the Dome of the Rock was built on the site of the rock from which he made his heavenly ascent.

The ensuing three centuries of Muslim reign was largely benevolent, and Christians and Jews were allowed free access to their places of worship, until 969 when Jerusalem was taken over by the Egyptian **Fatimids**, who had all churches and synagogues destroyed. In 1078 the city was captured by the more hostile **Seljuk Turks** and was closed to Christians and Jews.

The Byzantine Empire felt threatened as pilgrims returned with stories of persecution and the desecration of holy sites in Jerusalem. Pope Urban II called for a **Crusade** to re-open Jerusalem, and the forces of Europe mobilised. In fact the Fatimid Dynasty, who showed more tolerance to Christians and Jews, retook the city from the Seljuks in 1098. None the less, in the following year the Crusaders, led by Godfrey de Bouillon, fell upon Jerusalem in an orgy of slaughter. It is said that the streets ran red with Muslim blood; the city's Jews, regarded as Christ-killers by the fanatical Christian armies, fared no better, and many were burned alive in their synagogues.

The Crusaders stayed for some 88 years before they were deposed in 1187 by the legendary ruler of Egypt, **Saladin**, who magnanimously allowed Christians to remain and Jews to return. The division of the city into its present four quarters dates from this time.

Saladin's dynasty, the **Ayyubids**, controlled Jerusalem for the next 40 years until, in 1229, the city passed briefly, by treaty, to Holy Roman Emperor **Frederick II**. He was unable to prevent the massacre of its Christians by Turks, however, and in 1260 the **Mameluke** dynasty of Egypt took charge. They stayed for three centuries, largely ignoring the city, which during this period stagnated to something of a backwater. Their main legacy to the city is the impressive architecture on Temple Mount and in the Muslim Quarter.

In 1516 the Mamelukes were defeated by the **Ottoman Turks**. Their most enlightened

The city walls built by Suleiman the Magnificent in the 16C today provide a good vantage point for tourists on the Ramparts Walk.

leader was **Suleiman the Magnificent** (1520-66), who briefly returned prosperity to the city, his mission being to build the city walls and gates that we see today. After his death, however, Jerusalem again lapsed into obscurity and spent the next 300 years or so as a forgotten outpost of the Ottoman Empire.

In the latter part of the 19C many Jews of the Diaspora (*see* p.12) began making their way back to Israel, fleeing from persecution in Europe. The concept of **Zionism**, Israel as a homeland for the Jewish people, began to take shape. From 1860 the first real building developments took place outside the Old City walls, with their names, such as the German Colony and the Russian Compound, reflecting their founders.

The Early 20C

The Ottoman Empire, by now on its last legs, sided with Germany in the First World War, and following the Allied victory the British marched into the city in 1917 to begin the period of rule known as the **British Mandate**. In the early years, Jerusalem flourished under the British, as modern schools, hospitals and neighbourhoods were built. But during the course of the war the British had made certain territorial promises to both Arabs and Jews, in return for helping to oust the Turks. It soon became clear that the promises to both parties could not be accommodated. Following **pogroms** in Russia, Jewish immigration boomed, but just as the Promised Land beckoned, the increasingly alarmed resident Palestinian population reacted angrily. Violence flared regularly between the two sides, with riots and sectarian murders commonplace. The British tried to keep the lid on the situation by initially imposing controls on Jewish immigration, then completely blocking it. By now, both sides were attacking the British as well as each other.

Two Jewish **underground movements**, the Irgun, led by future prime minister Menachem Begin, and the Hagana, were formed to smuggle in immigrants and also to fight a guerrilla war against the British. By the 1930s the situation for Jews abroad, particularly in Germany, was desperate, yet still the British immigration blockade continued.

Post Second World War

Even as the horrors of the **Holocaust** were just being laid bare to the world, the suffering of the Jewish people continued, with Jewish immigration restrictions still in place. This shameful chapter in British-Israeli relations is recounted in Leon Uris's novel (later a famous film) *Exodus*. In 1946 the King David Hotel – commandeered as a British headquarters in Jerusalem – was bombed by the Zionist Irgun movement, with the loss of 91 lives. Jews continued to beat the blockade, and by 1947 the 600 000 Jews in Palestine outnumbered Arabs by three to one. The exhausted British passed their 'Palestinian problem' over to the UN to sort out and in 1947, after nine months of debate, the General Assembly voted to **partition** Palestine into Jewish and Arab states, with Jerusalem as an international city, open to both but belonging to neither. Arabs rioted in protest throughout Palestine and beyond, and fighting broke out resulting in deaths on both sides.

Statehood and Wars

The State of Israel was no sooner declared when the British withdrew, on 14 May 1948, than it was plunged into war. This **War of Independence**, waged against the combined force of five Arab states, lasted for seven months and cost around 6 000 Jewish lives. As in present-day Nicosia, on Cyprus, a 'Green Line' and a buffer zone was drawn up and policed by the UN, with West Jerusalem under Israeli control, and East Jerusalem (including the Jewish Quarter of the Old City, and access to the Western, or Wailing, Wall) under the Jordanian forces.

This divided city maintained an uneasy existence, with occasional violent incidents, for 19 years. In 1956 Israel was again at war, this time with Egypt over the nationalisation of the Suez Canal, though Jerusalem remained unaffected. Then in 1967 came Israel's finest military hour. As the combined armies of Egypt, Syria, Jordan and Iraq massed on her borders, the Israeli Air Force destroyed the air forces of each of her enemies in a pre-emptive strike. Without air cover, the Arabs were helpless and the **Six-Day War** was quickly won. The Jordanians were driven out of Jerusalem, and Israel annexed the West Bank. The Jewish Quarter was rebuilt, the Old City repaved and other rebuilding undertaken in an attempt to create a unified city that could never again be partitioned.

An Israeli tourist policeman chats with a Greek Orthodox priest outside the Holy Sepulchre Church.

The Present

Since 1987 the country has undergone
several traumas: the Palestinian *Intifada*
(uprising) in the West Bank; Iraqi scud
missiles (which thankfully caused little
damage) in the 1991 **Gulf War** – without
retaliation; the **assassination** of prime
minister Yitzhak Rabin by a Jew opposed to
the Arab peace treaty, in Tel Aviv in 1995.
There has also been some good news, most
notably the 1993 **peace accord** between
Israel and the Palestine Liberation
Organisation (PLO), and the 1994 **peace
agreement** with Jordan. However, recent
events have shown that the tricky peace
process has some way to go. Despite the
negotiations at Camp David in the summer
of 2000, under the aegis of President
Clinton, the tragic events of the autumn
have shown that the status of Jerusalem
remains one of the most intractable
problems in the modern world.

PEOPLE AND CULTURE

Despite its often incredible sense of national
purpose and unity, Israel is a state of very
many peoples and cultures. Jerusalem, in
particular, reflects much of this diversity.
Here are three of its main groupings.

Orthodox Jews

Orthodox Jews are the keepers of the faith.
They make up around one-third of the
Israeli population but have political
influence well in excess of this. Ultra-
Orthodox and Hasidic Jews are the
guardians of Judaism – fiercely conservative,
pious and ideological. Most refuse to fight
for the country (on ideological grounds),

An Orthodox Jew at the Wailing Wall.

which causes much friction with non-Orthodox Jews.

Traditionally of East European origin, their distinguishing dress is taken from late-18C Europe: for men a black trilby hat on top of a skull cap (*yarmulke*) or a fur hat on the Sabbath, long black coat, black trousers or breeches, sidelocks and beard. For the full range, take a look at the fashions at the Wailing Wall.

While less Orthodox Jews favour some form of integration in the greater society, the Ultra-Orthodox keep very much to themselves, sometimes forming virtually closed communities such as Me'a She'arim in Jerusalem. Ultra-Orthodox women cover all but their hands and face, and the only men they can be in an enclosed room with are close relatives.

Typically, visitors will see or experience few Jewish customs as these are mostly private religious rituals, confined to the home, but the Sabbath (Shabbat) does impinge on everyone. It lasts from sundown Friday to sundown Saturday, and is a day of general rest, when no activity whatsoever may be undertaken by an Orthodox Jew. During this time, the streets of Jerusalem are very quiet. The only other common Jewish practice that impinges on visitors is *kashrut*, the dietary laws of *kosher* (meaning clean) eating (*see* p.97).

Sabras

Sabra is a nickname given to those born in Israel as opposed to those who have emigrated to Israel. Typically young, realistic, without illusions, straight-talking, confident in themselves and proud of the State, Sabras work hard, play hard and are often mature beyond their years compared to their Western counterparts. Perhaps when you are surrounded by hostile neighbours, live with the daily threat of internal terrorism and have the huge responsibility of caring for the world's holiest places, then you have to be tough simply to survive. The nickname comes from the sabra fruit, hard and prickly on the outside, but soft on the inside.

Sabras come from a wide range of ethnic backgrounds, both Ashkenazi (North European) and Sephardi. The latter term originally meant of Spanish origin but has now developed into a wider catch-all term, encompassing Oriental Jews from North Africa, Yemen, the Middle East and the Eastern Mediterranean – in fact almost anyone of non-Northern European origin. During the first decades of the Israeli State, Ashkenazi Jews have occupied the leading jobs in Israeli society. But now the two groups have mixed and the Sephardi Jews are to be found in all layers of Israeli leadership. It is estimated that one-third of all Sabras are in fact a marriage of Ashkenazi and Sephardi, which often makes for a fascinating hybrid of national characteristics, social background and physical features. Young Sabras, of both sexes, are some of the most beautiful people on earth. You can spot them almost anywhere in West Jerusalem, particularly around the cafés and bars of the Midrahov in the New City.

Arabs

The Arabs of Israel – and Jerusalem has a large community in the Muslim Quarter and East Jerusalem – are in a very difficult position. As part of a nation which has fought three wars against their neighbours, they have the choice to fight alongside Israelis against their brother Arabs, to be a powerless spectator or to rebel and become an enemy of the State. The Arabs are exempt from national service. They may volunteer to serve, but few do, and this in itself is a major excluding factor from the mainstream society. The army (and air force) is Israel's great uniting factor, the one body that pulls together Jews from every nation and every background and gives them the ultimate shared experience and common purpose. In jobs, housing, state benefits and many other social matters, Arabs are discriminated against on a daily basis.

Cultures mingle in the busy David Street market.

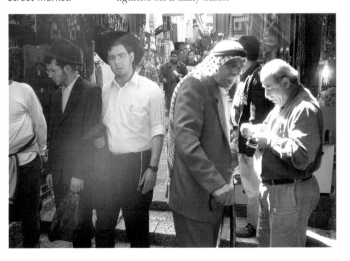

MUST SEE

📖 *This denotes a place of great religious significance.*

📖 Dome of the Rock

One of the great buildings of the world.
Beneath its glowing golden dome is a heady
mixture of Koranic script, simple yet
marvellously effective geometric patterns,
and radiant yet restrained colours.

📖 The Western ('Wailing') Wall

The sheer size of the ancient wall (it towers

15m/50ft high), the crowds of traditionally garbed Orthodox Jews who flock across the gleaming wide plaza, and the backdrop of the golden Dome of the Rock peeking above the Wall, make this one of the city's most compelling spectacles.

The Mount of Olives provides the backdrop to the Church of All Nations and the Garden of Gethsemane.

Church of the Holy Sepulchre

The holiest place in Christendom is big, noisy, confusing, and not at all as you might have expected. A good guide can navigate you through the crowds, point out the last five Stations of the Cross, and perhaps even find you a moment of peace in its side chapels. Don't miss the Ethiopian Compound on the roof.

The Israel Museum★★★

The country's finest collection of archaeological finds, with the star exhibit being the striking Dead Sea Scrolls exhibition, the **Shrine of the Book**. But there is lots here besides, including excellent art and ethnography sections. Take a guided tour to get you started.

The Citadel (King David's Tower)★★

A city landmark, this beautifully restored 14C fortress houses the **Museum of the History of Jerusalem** in David's Tower, and is the best place to get to grips with Jerusalem's long and fascinating history.

Mount of Olives

The **views★★★** across to the Old City from the 'promenade' in front of the beautiful **Church of All Nations** have launched a thousand postcards. Despite the crowds, there is generally a hush in the adjacent **Garden of Gethsemane**.

St James's Cathedral★★
Neglected by most visitors, this ancient Armenian church exudes a sense of time past. It is just the place to find that mystical atmosphere which you have come to Jerusalem to experience.

Yad VaShem★★★
It may be tempting to leave Yad VaShem off your itinerary, as it is undoubtedly a terrible and traumatic reminder of man's capacity for evil, but a visit to Israel would be incomplete without it.

The Dead Sea★★★
One of the natural wonders of the world and the only place on earth where even non-swimmers can float effortlessly in the water. Go the whole hog, slap mud all over, rinse it off and give your skin that Dead Sea glow!

Masada★★★
The Siege of Masada is the embodiment of the Israeli pledge of death before dishonour. Never was there a more glorious defeat, nor such a dramatic stage. It makes a deep impression on all who come here.

THE OLD CITY★★★

The walled Old City, tightly packed into one square kilometre, is Jerusalem as it has been since the Middle Ages. Indeed, for many visitors this *is* Jerusalem. History and religion seep from its very stones. It is not a place for the claustrophobic, and such is the density of its major sites that if you were really determined you could visit the holiest shrine in Christendom, the holiest place in the Jewish world, and the third most sacred

The narrow streets of the Old City are clustered within the confines of Suleiman the Magnificent's 16C walls.

shrine in the Muslim world, all within less than half an hour. Tensions do occasionally run high but, given this cheek-by-jowl existence and the rainbow of religious persuasions present, the miracle is that for the vast majority of the time its 20 000 people do in fact co-habit very peacefully.

The pale gold limestone walls, which stretch for some 4km (2.5 miles) around the city, date from the 16C when they were built by King Suleiman the Magnificent. You can walk around approximately three-quarters of them on the **Ramparts Walk** (*see* p.14). For security reasons you are not allowed on the

section overlooking Temple Mount. There are three entrance points to the Ramparts Walk: at Jaffa Gate; close by, near the Citadel; and at the Damascus Gate. You can exit at any gate. It is a good way to get your bearings, even though you are not high enough to get really good views down into the jumbled roofscape. Attacks on lone tourists have occurred on this walk, and women should not go unaccompanied.

The Old City is divided into four quarters – Armenian, Jewish, Muslim and Christian. There are no formal divisions between these areas; the dress of the inhabitants and/or the architecture will tell you when you have entered the Jewish or Muslim quarters, but the Armenian and Christian areas are less distinctive.

The ancient Jaffa Gate still marks the entrance to the Old City for many Western visitors today.

Armenian Quarter

Our tour begins in the **Armenian Quarter**, at the **Jaffa Gate★** (EY), the main western entrance to the Old City. Just inside on the left is the tourist office, and a whole host of unofficial guides (whom you should politely discourage). By all means consider a guided tour, but don't be scared to do the city by yourself. It may look daunting initially, and no doubt you will get lost, but it is a small area, safe (certainly by day), largely free of the hassle associated with the East, and populated by a good number of English-speaking people who can usually point you in the right direction.

26

Inside the Jaffa Gate

The striking picture-book fortress immediately right of the Jaffa Gate is known as the **Citadel★★** (El Qal'a), or **King David's Tower** (EY), after its landmark minaret added by Suleiman the Magnificent between 1635 and 1655 (its 'King David' attribution is a historical aberration). The hill site has been strategically important throughout history, and has been fortified by successive rulers since the Hasmoneans in the 2C BC. It was once the seat and palace of Herod the Great, who strengthened the Hasmonean walls and added towers, one of which, the **Phasael Tower** (albeit much rebuilt), still survives and offers good **views★**. The Citadel **ramparts** you see today date mostly from the 14C. The Citadel is home to the **Museum of**

Set on high ground, the Citadel has been fortified and fought over throughout the city's history.

the History of Jerusalem★★ and,
appropriately, Herod's tower houses an
entertaining introductory film. You are free
to wander around the beautifully restored
rooms, set on multiple levels, and the lovely
grounds. Unusually for a historical museum,
there is not a single article of any antiquity
but its displays are inventive, intelligent and
illuminating. Come back in the evening for
a sound and light performance (*see* p.104).

From the Citadel, the vast majority of
visitors plunge headlong into the colourful
souqs of David Street, unaware that the most
beautiful and atmospheric church in all
Jerusalem is less than 100m away. Turn right
into Armenian Orthodox Patriarchate Road
and you will find the hidden gem that is
St James's Cathedral★★ (EZ) – experience
the unforgettable beauty of the Armenian
choir's singing in the side chapels during a
service (open only for services: Mon-Fri

*As the hooded
and robed priests of
the Armenian
Cathedral of
St James chant their
prayers through
clouds of incense,
you will feel the
centuries slipping
away and a shiver
run down your
spine.*

Novice priests
celebrate Mass in
the Armenian
Cathedral of
St James.

6.30-7.15am, 3-3.45pm, and Sat-Sun 2.30-4pm). It dates largely from the 11C but feels much older and is of modest size, despite its cathedral status. Don't miss the beautiful 18C tiles (an Armenian speciality) which grace the side chapels. As you go out of the Cathedral, notice the typical Armenian stone crosses with different designs sculptured on the wall of the courtyard; these crosses are called *khatchhars*.

Like the Cathedral, the history of the Armenians is little known to most outsiders. Around AD 303, Armenia was the first nation to embrace Christianity and a delegation was sent to Jerusalem in the 5C. They have been here ever since, albeit now numbering only 1 500. Like the Jews, they suffered terribly in the 20C, losing over 1.5 million people in the Turkish genocide of 1915. Notices posted around the Armenian Quarter inform visitors of this 'forgotten holocaust'. While in the Armenian quarter, it is worth visiting the **Armenian Museum**★ (Edward & Helen Mardigian Museum) (EZ) which is installed in an old seminary not far from St James's Cathedral, further along the same street that leads to Zion Gate. Among the exhibits on display are moving documents and photos of the Armenian Genocide, ceramics from the Turkish region of Kütaya, pottery, religious jewellery and part of a mosaic discovered in the Armenian garden. The site is very pleasant in itself, with its **courtyard**★ surrounded with colonnades partly covered with vegetation and background medieval Armenian music to soothe the soul.

Beautiful Armenian tiles decorate the side chapels of St James's Cathedral.

The Temple

According to the *Books of Kings*, the First Temple was built by King Solomon in the 10C BC, to hold the Ark of the Covenant. It survived for 400 years, until its destruction by King Nebuchadnezzar of Babylon in 586 BC, when the Jews were taken into captivity. They were allowed to return 50 years later, and built the Second Temple around 515 BC (*see* p.9) This more modest temple, later embellished and restored by Herod, stood for 600 years until it was destroyed in AD 70 by the Romans, who left no trace of the actual Temple building. The only thing that remains from the Temple grounds is part of the retaining Western 'Wailing' Wall (*see* p.39).

Temple Mount now covers the site of the destroyed Temples and it is thought that the Ark of the Covenant and other priceless biblical treasures are still buried beneath here, on the spot known as the 'Holy of Holies'. No one knows its exact location, and its importance to the Jewish people may be gauged by the fact that Orthodox Jews are forbidden to venture anywhere on Temple Mount, less they should accidentally stand above the site – which is forbidden to all but the High Priest – and profane it with their presence.

There are various places where you can get a three-dimensional idea of what the Temple would have looked like. The easiest way is to visit

the **Museum of the History of Jerusalem**, in the Citadel (*see* p.28), which features a hologram and a detailed large-scale model. Or you can join a guided tour into the controversial tunnel that has been dug underneath the Western Wall (advance booking essential; ☎ 02 627 1333). An auditorium down here also has a detailed model of the Second Temple. Largest of all the models is the **Jerusalem Model★**, built on a scale of 1:50, showing the whole of the Old City around the time of Christ. It is set in the gardens of the Holyland Hotel, 4km (2.5 miles) south-west of the Old City (bus nos 21 or 21a). Another intriguing interpretation of this era is offered by the **Museum of Temple Treasures**, in the Jewish Quarter, which displays reconstructed Temple objects.

Jerusalem Model of the Second Temple, at the Holyland Hotel.

EXPLORING JERUSALEM

Make your way back to the Citadel and turn left into **David Street★** (Sūq el Bazar) (EFY), which tumbles quite steeply into a covered warren of atmospheric souqs, dimly lit by bare bulbs. Not surprisingly, those nearest the entrance cater for tourists, but as you get further in there are plenty of shops for locals, with pungent spices, bright materials and tempting food aromas (*see* p.52). You may be hassled by stallholders eager to persuade you to buy their goods, but by Middle Eastern standards the sales pitch is quite resistible, so don't be put off exploring and spend a little time soaking up the sights and sounds.

Lose yourself in the sights, sounds and smells of the exotic souqs, such as the cotton market seen here.

📖 Temple Mount/Harem esh-Sharif

David Street runs into the **Muslim Quarter** (*see* p.51) and becomes Bāb es Silsila Road (FY), which leads to **Temple Mount** (GY). Known to Muslims as **Haram esh-Sharif** (The Noble Sanctuary), it is surrounded by three of its own walls (part of which is the famous Western Wall) and is enclosed entirely by the south-eastern section of the Old City wall. This site is of utmost importance to both Jews and Muslims, and is the most contentious parcel of ground in all the Holy Land.

For Muslims, Harem esh-Sharif is the point from which the prophet Mohammed

The magnificent Dome of the Rock dominates Temple Mount.

(the founder of Islam) ascended to Heaven on the Night Journey described in the *Koran*. For Jews it is sacred as the site of the First and Second Temples (*see* p.30). Christians, too, venerate Temple Mount, as it was here on the place known as Mount Moriah that the angel stayed the hand of Abraham as he prepared to sacrifice his son, Isaac (Muslims in fact claim that Mohammed is a descendant of Abraham).

When on Bāb es Silsila Road (HaShalshelet), you can either take the Western Wall Road which leads to the police control point that allows you to enter the large esplanade in front of the Western Wall (*see* p.39), or take on the left a vaulted street with steps down to another police control point, before going through a tunnel leading into the western part of the esplanade. There are several entrances to the Temple Mount itself, but non-Muslims should enter only by the **Bāb el-Maghariba** (Gate of the Moors) (GY) at the southern end of the Western Wall (non-Muslims can leave by any gate, but need to pass through a special police check point when entering).

By contrast with the bustling streets outside, and in spite of the heavy presence of armed Israeli soldiers (designed to deter extremist attacks), Temple Mount is an oasis of peace. From the dark entrance tunnel you step out into a large, bright, airy stone plaza, about the size of two football pitches, fringed with some delightful pieces of classical **Islamic architecture**, including fountains such as the beautiful Mameluke **fountain★** of the Sultan Qait Bey, on the western side of Temple Mount, a fine marble **minbar★** near the Al-Aksa Mosque, arches and several small domed structures.

Hearing the plaintive call to prayer of the muezzin on Harem esh-Sharif, while gazing in awe at the perfect architectural beauty of the Dome of the Rock.

Its centrepiece is the fabulous **Dome of the Rock** (Qubbat es Sakhra), constructed 688-691 to overshadow the Church of the Holy Sepulchre. At the time, Jerusalem was the centre of the Muslim world, though today Mecca and Medina are rated as more important.

The Dome of the Rock is essentially a two-storey octagon, topped with a golden dome. For a time only gold-anodised aluminium, this has been restored to gold, thanks to King Hussein of Jordan. However, it is the building's brilliant decorative blue, white and yellow **tiles****, which line both inside and outside walls, that make it an Arabian

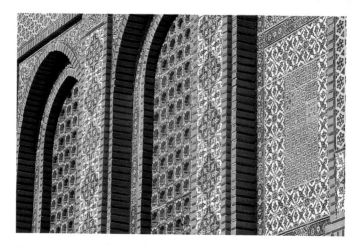

Nights fantasy. Koranic inscriptions adorn the wall below the dome.

Upon stepping inside, most visitors are taken aback to be greeted by an enormous meteorite-like rock, traditionally the very stone from which Mohammed ascended to Heaven, and on which Isaac had a narrow escape. If you have a guide, he will point out indents which are supposed to be the footprint of the Prophet and the fingerprints of the Archangel Gabriel, who is said to have held the rock steady for Mohammed. Many other relics and legends are associated with the rock, in both Muslim and Jewish lore. Perhaps the most extraordinary is that beneath the rock the waters of the Great Flood may still be heard roaring. Steps lead to a sacred cave below the rock, the **Well of Souls**, where the dead are said to pray twice a month.

Stepping outside the Dome of the Rock and down from the central plaza area, you

Exquisite ceramic tiles in shades of blue, turquoise and gold adorn the Dome of the Rock.

see Temple Mount extending for some 200m (650ft) north and south. Due east is the legendary **Golden Gate** (Sha'ar haRahamim) (GY), through which the Messiah will enter the city on the Day of Judgement. It has been sealed since the 7C and you are not allowed to approach it. Also note that the other outer edges of Temple Mount (not necessarily signed) may be off-limits on security grounds.

The other major site on Temple Mount is the **Al-Aksa Mosque** (Masjid el Aqsa), whose large silver dome seems to defer to the gold of its neighbour, though in fact the Al-Aksa is the most important mosque in the country. This is a working place of worship, while the Dome of the Rock is more symbolic. Mohammed visited the site of the Al-Aksa too, tethering his horse here before his Night Journey. The mosque was originally built in 705, but today's structure dates mostly from the 11C, when the Crusaders

The 14C Al-Kas (The Cup) fountain, used for washing before prayer, stands in front of the Al-Aksa Mosque.

A large collection of beautiful Korans are displayed in the Islamic Museum.

The Western (Wailing) Wall – the most sacred of all Jewish sites.

used it as their headquarters, and was later improved and embellished by Saladin. Parts of the interior are quite modern. It is an impressive large space with some splendid **decoration**★★ – a beautiful carved painted roof, huge marble pillars and lavish Persian rugs – in parts echoing the Dome of the Rock, although it lacks the atmosphere of the Dome and should be visited first so that it does not suffer by comparison. The same can be said for the adjacent **Islamic Museum**, which contains some fine pieces but is uninspiringly presented (look for the medieval and Ottoman **Korans**★ in the manuscript section).

A combined ticket, purchased from the kiosk on Temple Mount, allows entrance to the Dome of the Rock, Al-Aksa Mosque and the Islamic Museum. Opening times are Sat-Thur 8am-3pm (last entry), but there is an hour closure for lunchtime prayers: 11.30am-12.30pm winter; 12.30-1.30pm summer. Beware of unofficial guides who, acting as officials, try to relieve you of your ticket prematurely and then attach themselves to you.

📖 Western (Wailing) Wall

Immediately adjacent to Temple Mount but not accessible from it, is the famous **Western Wall** (also known as The Wailing Wall, HaKotel Hama'aravi) (GY) – you can leave Temple Mount through the Bāb es Silsila and walk back up Bāb es Silsila Road, turning left again into the security tunnel leading to the esplanade. The Wall is open 24 hours.

The so-called 'wailing' is a ritual mourning for the destruction of Solomon's Temple (*see* p.30). In fact the Wall never was

Traditional horn-blower in front of the Western Wall.

part of the actual Temple building, merely a retaining support wall for the Temple complex. The lower parts date from 20 BC. What is important is that it makes a connection with the spirit of the Temple and is therefore the holiest place in the Jewish world. The Wall is both a shrine and a bulletin board to God. Men proceed to the prayer area on the left, women to the right; they pray, among other things, for the restitution of Jerusalem to the Jewish people, and push prayer notes on scraps of paper into the cracks between the massive stones. Gentiles may also approach the wall but men should cover their heads (cardboard skull caps are provided free).

The Wall is particularly atmospheric on a Friday afternoon just before the Sabbath and is also the only time you should not take photographs here. For the best views, and the classic photograph, go to the far end of the esplanade and climb the steps. You have now entered the Jewish Quarter.

Jewish Quarter

The Jewish Quarter is completely different in character from the rest of the Old City. It was virtually razed in the fighting of 1948 when it was captured and occupied by the Jordanians, who let it lie neglected until 1967 when Israel retook this part of the city. Huge amounts of investment poured in to make this the richest part of the Old City, and even today Palestinians are forbidden to live here. Gone are the narrow, dark alleyways and cramped living quarters. Instead there are light, airy squares and modern attractive houses, built in the 'Old Jerusalem style'. Gone too is the Old City hustle and bustle, and although the Jewish Quarter may lack atmosphere it is a good place to sit down and relax awhile. There are no major visitor attractions, but the area is dotted with minor sites, mostly of archaeological interest.

This graceful arch is as far as attempts to rebuild the Hurva Synagogue have got.

From the steps overlooking the Western Wall, follow the signposts to **The Burnt House** (FZ), to see how an upper-class family house would have looked around AD 70, just

before this part of the city was torched by the Romans. An audio-visual presentation sets the scene.

Close by, in similar vein and time period, is the **Wohl Archaeological Museum**★★ (FZ) which comprises the remains of six priests' houses. From the Wohl Museum exit, turn left, walk up Hayye'Olam Street and turn right into **Hurva Square**, the main gathering point of the Jewish Quarter. The graceful landmark arch you see is part of the ill-starred **Hurva Synagogue**. Completed in 1856 after over 150 years of on-off activity, it was destroyed in 1948. The arch was built in 1977 but, as with the original building, indecision and planning problems have led to a state of limbo.

Running directly behind the synagogue ruins is the main attraction of the Jewish Quarter, **The Cardo**★ (FY), which was the principal street of Roman Jerusalem. Lying well below the present street level, it has

Shopping the Roman way, in The Cardo, Roman Jerusalem's restored main street.

been beautifully restored and you can walk along a colonnaded section which actually dates from the Byzantine period. At the northern end are gift shops and the small but interesting **One Last Day Museum** (FY), which records the fall of the Jewish Quarter in 1948 through the lens of a *Life* magazine photographer. The Cardo leads back to David Street.

Via Dolorosa

From David Street take the Sūq el Attārin, which becomes the Sūq Khan ez-Zeit, as far as the **Via Dolorosa** (FXY). This famous street, also known as the Way of Sorrows, or Way of the Cross, is by tradition the route taken by Christ to his Crucifixion. Christian pilgrims may hire a cross from the Church of the Holy Sepulchre and walk the 500m or so in His footsteps. On Fridays at 3pm the Franciscan Fathers lead a procession.

There are 14 **Stations of the Cross** (i.e. points of significant event along the route), which begin to the east in the Muslim Quarter and finish in the Christian Quarter in the Church of the Holy Sepulchre. In fact the Via Dolorosa has been argued over and changed many times throughout the centuries. It goes through narrow streets in the Muslim Quarter, the level of which is a lot higher than it was thought to be at the time of Jesus. Even the direction of its route is a major point of contention. Given that Pontius Pilate would have stayed in Herod's palace, which was the Citadel, it seems more likely that it would have run west-east and not vice versa. All the Stations are marked by a wall plaque or similar marker but beware – the Via Dolorosa zigzags across the El-Wād Road (HaGay) between Stations III and V.

Stations I and II - Jesus is tried and condemned by Pilate in his Great Antonia Fortress (of which nothing remains), Jesus receives the Cross and is scourged. This is marked by the **Monastery of the Flagellation**, the **Chapel of Judgement**, and the **Convent of the Sisters of Zion** (FX). None of the buildings has any historical pedigree but all are open to visitors. The adjacent **Lithostrotos** (courtyard pavement) dates from Roman times and the inscriptions on the slabs were made by soldiers playing games. Below the Lithostrotos you can see the **Struthion**, a large water reservoir dug at the time of Herod and covered later with a vault in the time of Hadrian (AD 135) and transformed into a cistern over which the house has been erected. Spanning the Via Dolorosa at this point is the **Ecce Homo Arch★**, which dates from AD 135. Ecce Homo means 'Behold the Man', echoing Pilate's jeer. The arch continues inside the church belonging to the convent of the Sisters of Zion where its northern part, which is larger, can be seen.

Station III (junction of El-Wād Road) - Jesus falls; a small relief depicts the event.

Station IV - The most poignant Station, where Jesus sees his mother, Mary. In the Armenian church a footprint in the 5C mosaic floor is said to have been made by Mary.

Station V - Simon (the Cyrenian) is ordered to help Jesus with the Cross. Look out for the handprint of Jesus on the wall.

A priest carries the cross at Station III.

Station VI - Veronica wipes Jesus's face. The Chapel of St Veronica, which marks the spot, is in the care of a Greek Orthodox community and stands where the house of this woman was supposed to be. Veronica's famous cloth, said to bear Christ's likeness, is kept either at the Greek Orthodox Patriarchate (between Stations II and III but not open to the public) or at St Peter's, Rome – depending on whom you believe.

Station VII - Jesus falls again. This station is marked by a little Franciscan chapel, at the junction of Via Dolorosa and Sūq Khan ez-Zeit (FY).

Station VIII - Jesus tells the women, 'Do not weep for me but weep for yourselves and your children,' prophesying the destruction of the city in AD 70. This station, in Aqabat El Khanqa Street, is marked by a cross on the wall of a Greek monastery.

Station IX - Jesus falls for a third time. This station is indicated by a cross on a pillar on the left hand side of the entrance of the Coptic Orthodox Patriarchate and, bizarrely, is located on the same level as the roof of the Church of the Holy Sepulchre. The flat area which opens next door is the Ethiopian Compound (*see* p.50).

From here you can reach the Church of the Holy Sepulchre, going through two small superimposed Ethiopian chapels: the Deir es-Sultan Chapel to which the terrace gives access, and from there stairs take you down to a

An Egyptian Coptic priest at Station IX, by the Church of the Holy Sepulchre – note the cross on the pillar.

second chapel which opens on the entrance courtyard of the Holy Sepulchre.

Stations X to XIV are all inside the Church of the Holy Sepulchre. Turn immediately right and go upstairs to find: Station X, Jesus is stripped; Station XI, He is nailed to the Cross; Station XII, He dies on the Cross; Station XIII, He is taken down from the Cross. Station XIV is His tomb, the Holy Sepulchre. It can be found downstairs. Just look for the queue.

Christian Quarter

📖 The Church of the Holy Sepulchre (FY)

You come upon the holiest spot in Christendom almost by accident. It is virtually completely hemmed in by the warren of buildings around it and the only vista is that of its front entrance and tower.

There has been a church on this site since

From the outside, the Church of the Holy Sepulchre is a confusion of structures and levels.

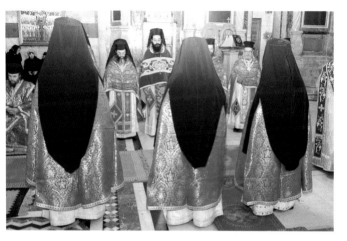

Greek Orthodox priests in the Church of the Holy Sepulchre.

AD 66 but it was first proclaimed as the site of the Crucifixion by St Helena, mother of the Emperor Constantine, in the 4C, when she found a piece of the True Cross in a cave nearby. Recent archaeological excavations have also revealed that in Roman times the site lay outside the city walls, confirming that executions and burials could have occurred here. Helena's church, built in 348, was destroyed in 614 and today's structure dates mostly from the 11C, a mix of Byzantine and Crusader styles.

The church interior is a hotchpotch, once memorably described as 'a cross between a building site and a used furniture depot', which reflects the fact that its joint stewards – Roman Catholics, Greek Orthodox, Armenian Orthodox, Syrian Orthodox, Ethiopians and Egyptian Copts – cannot seem to agree on a single thing. This encompasses both spiritual and secular matters, so that even the most minor repairs

Roman Catholics kiss the Stone of Unction.

and refurbishments are contentious enough
to lead to physical violence. Indicative of this
state of affairs is the fact that because none
of the Christian sects trusts the other, the
church key holder is a local Muslim family.

The first thing that you see when entering
the gloom is a slab, permanently awash with
a film of water, illuminated by eight hanging
lamps which, like mountaineers' flags,
proclaim the sovereignty of each of the
different Christian sects. Pilgrims soak up
the water and kiss the slab as this is the
Stone of Unction (or Anointment) the place
where, according to the Greeks, the Body of
Christ was removed from the Cross, or,
according to the Roman Catholics, anointed
before burial.

The claimed **site of the Crucifixion** is
reached upstairs to the right, marked by
three competing chapels and a cut-out
figure of Christ. Pilgrims go on all fours to
kiss the hole which the Cross was once
supposed to occupy. Far from being a place
for piety or quiet reflection, it is usually
occupied by a noisy camera-flashing scrum.
Go back down the stairs and you can see

(behind glass) the point at which the Cross entered the solid rock of **Golgotha**, or **Calvary**.

The actual **Holy Sepulchre** is, like most of the church, also something of a surprise. Sited underneath the main dome, the slab on which Christ's body lay is enclosed by an *aedicule*, a bizarre, highly decorated, black square Victorian-Gothic-looking kiosk, designed in the 19C. It can hold only up to four people at a time and there is usually a long line of pilgrims waiting to enter. As you are waiting you may hear the various sects chanting, not in harmony, but in competition with each other. Visitors, meanwhile, shuffle aimlessly to and fro, trying to make sense of their surroundings. If you want to explore more of the church you really need a guide.

To escape the cacophony and to discover the church's greatest surprise, leave by the front entrance and on your left, next to a flight of stairs, go through a small door leading into an Ethiopian chapel. Go up to the first floor where there is another Ethiopian chapel, at the back of which is

Mosaic at the entrance to the Church of the Holy Sepulchre.

access to the **Ethiopian Compound**. This large flat area is actually located on the roof of St Helena's Chapel, whose cupola can be seen in the middle of the terrace. The compound is home to the Ethiopian order of monks who were evicted from the main church in one of the many inter-denominational rows which happened below, but it is also shared with Egyptian Copts. There is no love lost between these sects, as both claim this patch as their own, but at least to the casual visitor it seems peaceful and quiet up here. Oblivious of the few tourists who make it this far, old men dressed in *jellabahs* and traditional headgear shuffle about their business, passing in and out of domed, whitewashed mud-hut cells. In the space of a few seconds, it seems that you have been transported from Jerusalem to Africa.

A Palestinian vendor sells cool Carob drinks outside the Damascus Gate.

Immediately south of the Church of the Holy Sepulchre (leave the church compound, turn right, then right again, passing St Alexander's Church) is the small area known as the **Muristan**. Its name derives from the Persian for hospices, which once proliferated here in the shadow of the Church of the Holy Sepulchre, beside various religious establishments. The latter are still here, as are several cafés which make a convenient place to rest awhile. Among these is the **Roof Café Papa Andrea's**. From its terrace on the roof, there are panoramic **views★** over the domes of the Holy Sepulchre and the Dome of the Rock. For the best view of the Church, and excellent **views★★** over the Old City in general, climb the tower of the landmark **Lutheran Church** (FY).

Muslim Quarter★

For Western visitors this is the most exotic and atmospheric part of the city. The entrance to this Quarter and the main focus of activity is around the impressive **Damascus Gate★** (Sha'ar Shekhem) (FX), the most handsome and busiest of all the city gates. Take a seat on the steps just outside – it's the best location in town for people-watching – or, after having passed through the gate into the Old City, stop on your left at the **Gate Café**, another good spot for people-watching while enjoying a long fresh orange juice.

Just inside the gate there is a real buzz, with old-fashioned moneychangers, pancake makers, street vendors (Muslim women simply plonk themselves and their fresh vegetables down on the busy pavement) and barrow boys selling bananas and other fruits. Note the Arab tourist offices offering excursions to Palestinian refugee camps alongside the more usual tourist attractions. It's all quite safe, though do be discrete when taking photos.

The **El-Wād Road** (FXY)

The bustle of activity takes on new pace inside the Damascus Gate.

leads directly from the gate all the way to the Western Wall. Close to the gate it is joined at a fork by Sūq Khan ez-Zeit Street, which is the dividing line with the Christian Quarter. As long as you keep these two main thoroughfares in mind, you should not get too lost.

Sūq Khan ez-Zeit (FXY) is a busy, bustling street lined with shops, mostly catering for locals, but none the less providing intriguing window-shopping for Western visitors. Jerusalem's most colourful shopping is to be enjoyed in the area known as the **Central Souqs★★** (FY), where Sūq Khan ez-Zeit splits into three other souqs, El-Attārin, El-Khawajat and El-Lahhamin, all of which end at David Street. The first two once sold spices, perfumes and gold and are now devoted mainly to clothes. The latter is the butchers' souq and should be avoided by visitors of a squeamish disposition.

As a complete contrast to the buzzing souqs, make your way along the El-Wād Road, then turning left follow the Via

The ruins of the Pools of Bethesda are next to the 12C Crusader Church of St Anne.

Dolorosa east towards **St Stephen's Gate**★★ (also known as **Lions' Gate**) (GX). Just before the gate are the two **Churches of St Anne**, dedicated to the mother of the Virgin Mary. The first is the Greek Orthodox, which is of no great architectural merit, though its underground chapel claims to be the birthplace of the Virgin Mary and last resting place of St Anne and her husband, St Joachim. The adjacent **Catholic Church of St Anne** is recognised as one of the finest examples of a Crusader church in the Holy Land. Built in 1140 in simple Romanesque style, it became an Islamic seminary when the Crusaders lost Jerusalem. It fell into ruin over the centuries, until it was given to the French Catholics in the 19C in gratitude for their support in the Crimean War, and was restored to its former beauty. In addition to its **architectural worth**★★, it is noted for its excellent acoustics, but is visited by pilgrims because it is said to lie on top of the house where Mary and her parents lived.

Next door are the impressive **Pools of Bethesda**★ where, according to St John, Jesus told the crippled man to get up and walk. It is thought that the pools were built in 200 BC to supply water to the Temple, but the lowest levels of these two giant pools have now been excavated to a depth of some 16m (50ft) and have been shown to date back to the 8C BC.

The excavations of the Pools of Bethesda – the waters were said to have medicinal powers after Jesus healed a sick man here.

EAST JERUSALEM

Most visitors get their first taste of East Jerusalem outside the **Damascus Gate★** (FX) (*see* p.51). This is the Palestinian Arab part of town, with the hustle and bustle of the Muslim Quarter spilling well beyond the city walls. Stretching from the Old City walls up to the affluent Arab neighbourhood of Sheikh Jarrah, the Nablus Road (also called Derekh Shekhem) (FX) and Salah ed-Din are the central thoroughfares running through this lively, distinctly Middle Eastern area. It has its own way of life, its own food, music, shops, buses, newspapers and public utilities. To the visitor, it can seem somewhat shabby in comparison with the modern shopping malls and cosmopolitan Midrahov of West Jerusalem, which receives the lion's share of the city's spending, but try to spend at least half a day or so here (remember that the Muslim day of rest is Friday).

Immediately below the Damascus Gate on Sultān Suleimān Road are the excavations known as **Solomon's Quarries**, which go back over 200m (655ft) below the Old City.

Peace and harmony radiate from the Garden Tomb – the true Golgotha or not is not really the issue here, for as it is written on the spot, 'He is not here for He is risen.'

Legend has it that slaves dug here for stone for the First Temple, and you can walk back for part of the way into these atmospheric red tunnels. They are also known as **Zedekiah's Caves**, after the story that Zedekiah, the last King of Judah, used this as his escape route from the invading Babylonians.

Cross the busy Sultān Suleimān Road opposite the Damascus Gate and walk up Nablus Road past the rumbling, horn-blaring buses and taxis overflowing from the frenetic Nablus Road Bus Station. After a few metres on the right is the **Garden Tomb** (DU) (closed Sunday). In stark contrast to the adjacent hullabaloo, this is probably the most peaceful spot in central Jerusalem. Refuting the long-held theory that the Church of the Holy Sepulchre was Christ's last resting place, the idea for this alternative tomb began in the late 19C and was popularised by General Gordon, of Khartoum fame. This beautiful, tranquil, flower-filled garden is run today by the Anglican Church, and gently-spoken volunteers will tell you its full history, beginning the tour by overlooking a hill which bears a striking resemblance to the skull-shaped Golgotha. There is an ancient cistern to see, and of course a tomb, cut into the rock, which at one time was thought to have dated from around the 1C. Sadly, for those visitors who would like to think that this charming bucolic spot was indeed the true place of Jesus' burial, archaeologists have dated the tomb to the 5C AD, and today the site is given little credence by most authorities.

Further along Nablus Road you will come to another piece of Jerusalem with strong

Experience elegance and style in the historic courtyard restaurant of the American Colony Hotel.

English connections – the **Cathedral of St George** (DT), a handsome Perpendicular-style church built in 1910. Seat of the Anglican Archbishop of Jerusalem, the complex comes complete with English-style gardens, a guesthouse and a school.

Keep on walking, past the sign which points to the **Tombs of the Kings** (behind St George's Cathedral compound, in Salah ed-Din Road), first thought to be the tombs of the Kings of Judah but subsequently proved to belong to Helena, a 1C Mesopotamian queen who converted to Judaism and travelled to Jerusalem in AD 45. You then come to the **American Colony** (DT). The 'colony' was founded by an American evangelist in the late 19C and at its heart is the famous **American Colony Hotel**. Dating from 1860 and converted from the palace of a Turkish pasha, it is probably the most atmospheric place to stay in all Jerusalem (*see* p.94). The hotel guest book is a veritable Who's Who of the 1940s and 1950s, from Lawrence of Arabia to Lauren Bacall, and over the years it has been a meeting place (sometimes in secret) for politicians and leaders from both sides of the Jerusalem divide. Above all, it is famed for its air of tolerance and mutual respect. Its courtyard is a perfect place for lunch.

Retrace your steps, turn left past the Tombs of the Kings into Salah ed-Din, return to the city walls (just east of the Damascus Gate) and turn left along Sultān Suleimān to the **Rockefeller Museum**★★ (GX), some 200m (220yds) east. This overlooked museum is dedicated to the city's archaeology and antiquities and contains an acclaimed collection. It is worth a visit if you have time, though its presentation is staid, and the Israel Museum (*see* p.72) is a better bet. Highlights include exquisitely carved wooden panels from the Al-Aksa Mosque, 12C Crusader lintels from the Church of the Holy Sepulchre, and stone ornamentation and frescoes from Hisham's Palace in Jericho. Enjoy the **views**★ over Mount Scopus (Har Ha-Zofim) and the Mount of Olives (Har Ha-Zetim) from the entrance, and escape the traffic noise in the central cloistered courtyard, with its refreshing tiled fountain.

The Rockefeller Museum is built round a cloistered courtyard pond.

EXPLORING JERUSALEM

📖 MOUNT OF OLIVES

Every visitor to Jerusalem makes a
pilgrimage to the Mount of Olives (Har Ha-
Zetim) (HY), if only for the marvellous
panorama*** of the Old City, with the
Dome of the Rock resplendent at its core. A
multitude of coaches and cars pull up on the
road in front of the Seven Arches Hotel each
day, to be greeted by souvenir salesmen,
unofficial guides and a cameleer offering
photo-opportunities astride his ship of the
desert. If you want to get a good
photograph, come in the early morning so
that the sun is at your back.

While there is usually no cause for alarm,
particularly on the crowded 'promenade'
stretch, there have been assaults on tourists
on the Mount of Olives and women in
particular should be vigilant while here and
should not visit alone.

Stretching all the way from the Mount of
Olives 'promenade' almost to the city walls is
the **Jewish Cemetery**, the biggest and oldest
of its kind in the world. According to
Zechariah, in the Old Testament, this is the
place where the Second Coming of the
Messiah will occur, when he will resurrect
the souls of the dead on Judgement Day and
then lead them through the **Golden Gate**
(GY) into the Old City. Among believers, the
cemetery is therefore deemed a very
desirable place to be buried, and for just
such an event the disgraced media tycoon
Robert Maxwell secured his place.

The Mount not only provides a tomb with
a view – it is home to some of the city's
holiest sites and, as elsewhere in the city,
there are many conflicting claims of custody.
If you intend visiting all the sites take the bus

The massive Jewish Cemetery, with the Old City, the Dome of the Rock and Al-Aksa Mosque beyond, viewed from the Mount of Olives.

(nos 37 or 75 to Al-Tur, from the Sultān Suleimān Road station, near the Damascus Gate) to the top of the hill, then walk down. If you take a taxi, ask the driver to drop you at the **Seven Arches Hotel**, which commands a panoramic **view★★★** of the city of Jerusalem. From here you go down a flight of steps and then walk down a steep road lined with walls and cypress trees leading you down the slope of the Mount of Olives. On your left is the **Tomb of the Prophets**, said to contain the remains of the Old Testament prophets, Zechariah, Haggai and Malachi, alongside some 50 other ancients. A guardian will lead you into this small 3 000-year-old catacomb with his flashlight for a tour of the tombs, though there is little to see. The main sites cluster at the bottom, around the Church of All Nations.

The top of the Mount is marked by three competing Churches of the Ascension. The **Russian Chapel of the Ascension**, at the very top, is a little off the main track, open only Tuesday and Thursday and so is omitted

The Lord's Prayer is inscribed in numerous languages on the walls of the cloister of the Church of the Pater Nostra.

from most visitors' itineraries. It marks the spot where the Christian Orthodox Church believe Jesus made his ascent into heaven. Below it is the **Church of the Ascension** (closed Sunday), with a high tower (45m/150ft) which offers **views★** as far as the Judean Desert. The smallest of the trio is the **Chapel** or **Mosque of the Ascension**. There has been a shrine here since the 4C though the present building, a tiny mosque, dates from the 11C. It is believed by both Christians and Muslims to be the spot from which Jesus, recognised in the Muslim world as a prophet, though not the Son of God, ascended to Heaven. As with Mohammed at the Dome of the Rock (*see* p.36), he is said to have left behind a footprint in the stone. Close by is the **Church of the Pater Noster** ('Our Father'). The present church dates from 1920, but was built over a crypt which incorporates the remains of a grotto in which Jesus is said to have taught His disciples the Christian world's most famous prayer, the Lord's Prayer. A previous basilica (Basilica Eleona) had been built by Helena, mother of Emperor Constantine, but was burnt down by the Persians in 614. Later the Crusaders built a chapel among the ruins. It was only in 1910 when excavations were carried out in the area that the chapel was rediscovered by the Dominicans. In the tiled **cloister★** near the church, the text of the Lord's Prayer is written in over 50 languages.

The tear-shaped Church of Dominus Flevit is a gem of modern design.

Continue downhill to the **Church of Dominus Flevit** ('The Lord Wept'), which recalls Luke's account (*19:41*) of Jesus weeping for what would become of Jerusalem. The most famous feature of the tear-shaped church, designed by the Italian architect Antonio Barluzzi and completed in 1955, is the cleverly framed **view★★** of the Old City through its leaded window, which features on many a picture postcard. During the church's construction, tombs were found dating back as far as the late Bronze Age (around 1500 BC), together with a 7C mosaic floor, parts of which are on display. From the pleasant gardens and terrace overlooking the Russian Church of Mary Magdalene there are interesting **views★★** over the Old City.

The gleaming gold onion-domes of the Church of Mary Magdalene are a Mount of Olives landmark.

The most beautiful building on the Mount of Olives, from the **exterior★** at least, is unquestionably the White Russian Orthodox **Church of Mary Magdalene**, built in 1885 by Tsar Alexander III. Although it is of minor relative importance, and is little visited, its seven golden onion-dome cupolas have become a picture-postcard symbol of the Mount. If you are around between Tuesday and Thursday, 10am-noon, do step inside to admire its fine **icons** and wall paintings. The Duke of Edinburgh's mother, Princess Alice of Greece, is buried here.

The church grounds claim to include part of the **Garden of Gethsemane**, though the popularly accepted site for this is below here, just above the main road. Despite the tour bus exhaust fumes which choke the air, and the constant scrum of people, the 'Garden' – a square of gnarled ancient olive trees (*geth-shemna* derives from 'olive press') – retains a peaceful air. Indeed, some of the trees have been dated as being over 2 000 years old, and it does not beggar belief to imagine this as the grove where Christ sought solace before he was betrayed by Judas (who subsequently hanged himself here from an olive tree) and arrested by the Romans. Alongside is the charming **Church of All Nations**, built in 1924 in a rare spirit of cooperation between 12 different countries. Also known as the Basilica of the Agony, it features a striking gold mosaic above the entrance (best seen in the afternoon when it is illuminated by the sun)

The classical Church of All Nations was designed by Antonio Barluzzi, who was also responsible for the Church of Dominus Flevit.

which depicts Christ's agony as he awaited betrayal. The attractive interior holds the rock claimed to be the very spot on which Jesus prayed and grieved.

A few metres from the church, on the main road, look for a small 15C cupola memorial. It marks the entrance to the 12C **Church of the Assumption** and the **Tomb of the Virgin Mary** (closed Sunday). It is said that the disciples interred Mary's body here, alongside Joseph, and Mary's parents, Anne and Joachim. However, the latter are also claimed to be buried at the Churches of St Anne (*see* p.53), while the better-known Virgin's tomb is the Church of the Dormition (*see* p.65). Whatever, this dark atmospheric **subterranean church**★, decked with smoky silver oil lamps and with its access via monumental stairs, is certainly worth a few minutes of your time.

Across the busy road from the Church of All Nations, a dirt track leads down into the **Kidron Valley** (Nahal Kidron), the valley between Temple Mount and the Mount of Olives which is home to a group of impressive **tombs**★ dating from around the 1C. The first that you come to, a burial cave with a frieze above, is the **Tomb of Jehosaphat**, the

The shrine at the Tomb of the Virgin Mary.

9C King of Judah. Next is the spectacular conical-roofed **Tomb/Pillar of Absalom**, speculated to be the last resting place of the son of King David. Adjacent is the **Tomb of the Bene Hezir**, a group of Jewish priests. This is also known as the Grotto of St James, after the story that James hid here following the arrest of Jesus. Close by, the square tomb with a pyramidal roof is said to be that of the Prophet **Zechariah**, though it too may be a monument to the Bene Hezir.

MOUNT ZION

The massive Tomb of Zechariah, in the Kidron Valley.

When Suleiman the Magnificent rebuilt the city walls, his architects unwisely left Mount Zion (EFZ) outside and it is said that he had them beheaded for the oversight. Lying immediately south of the city walls, Mount Zion is much less dramatic, and less romantic, than its name suggests. The term 'Zion' was used in the Old Testament meaning City of David, after Israel's first king. These days it is synonymous with Jerusalem and Israel as a whole, though latterly the term Zionism has taken on an unpleasant nationalistic overtone. However, the current Mount Zion, a hill of modest proportions, is not the original City of David at all – that lies to the east. Those relics located here which are associated with King David are therefore discredited by historians.

The hill is topped by the distinctive black conical dome of the **Church and Abbey of the Dormition** (EZ). Dormition means 'falling asleep', a euphemism for the death of the Virgin Mary, who 'fell asleep', supposedly upon this spot. The church was built in 1900 in an attractive modern neo-

Romanesque style that has won much acclaim. Inside, it has a bright, airy, peaceful atmosphere. The sanctuary has a beautiful gold-and-polychrome **mosaic*** of Mary and the baby Jesus, with the prophets of Israel below. The café here, which serves light lunches and alcoholic drinks, is a pleasant spot to take a break.

One of the lovely mosaics in the sanctuary of the Abbey of the Dormition.

Close by is the **Coenaculum** ('dining hall' in Latin), the location where it is alleged that the Last Supper took place. What you see today is an atmospheric, bare, vaulted Crusader hall, over a millennium younger than the actual event, but the sort of setting that Leonardo da Vinci would probably have enjoyed depicting. It's not the larger hall that marks the spot, but the smaller room off it.

Below the Coenaculum, in the same Crusader building, is **King David's Tomb** (DU). During the period 1948-67, when the Jordanians held the Western Wall, this was the main Jewish pilgrimage point, and even

The Room of the Last Supper, the Coenaculum.

today it is still of great importance. It is no great spectacle however, merely a casket, covered in a blue velvet cloth marked with the Star of David, in an unremarkable setting. Moreover, it is now generally agreed that this is probably not David's last resting place.

Opposite this building is the **Chamber of the Holocaust**, a small, eerie, candle-lit memorial to the Jews killed in Europe, containing relics of Auschwitz and other places. It's a thought-provoking place, but if you intend visiting Yad VaShem (*see* p.77) and time is short, you can give it a miss.

A few metres from here, in the Protestant Cemetery, is the grave of the man who saved an estimated 1 200 people from dying in the Holocaust – **Oskar Schindler**, immortalised in Steven Spielberg's film *Schindler's List*. Head downhill to the cemetery, go to the lower section and you will find it around four rows from the back, middle to right.

WEST JERUSALEM

West Jerusalem is a political as well as a geographic entity, and is almost entirely Jewish in its make-up. There are few sights but lots of places to eat, drink and shop, and for the Western visitor there are fascinating contrasts to be observed between the young secular Israelis basking in the café society of the Midrahov, and the Ultra-Orthodox Jews of Me'a She'arim.

The New City

Viewed from the bustling affluence of King George V Street (Ha-Melekh George V) (CU), the New City quarter of West Jerusalem is off-puttingly modern, created largely post-1967, encompassing high-rise hotels and office blocks, fast-food joints and the kind of shopping malls that you might find at home. It's a far cry from the Old City and a million miles from the traditional Middle East, though this, of course, is intentional. From

Ben Yehuda Street, centre of the nightlife scene in Jerusalem.

King George V Street, Ben Yehuda Street runs toward Zion Square (Kikkar Ziyyon) through the **Midrahov**, or pedestrianised area. Here, when the weather is warm, young Jerusalemites stroll and strut, and relax with a beer or coffee much as people do anywhere in the Mediterranean. This is also the main area for nightlife, such as it is, in Jerusalem (*see* p.102). The nicest thing about the Midrahov is that it takes in the old residential district of **Nahalat Shiva★**, which was built in the 1870s, an area full of small golden-stone houses in typical Jerusalem style. Many of these have been tastefully converted to restaurants, cafés, galleries and arts-and-crafts shops, and much of the best shopping is around here. Look along **Yoel Salomon Street** and **Yosef Rivlin Street** for some good examples (at the bottom of Rivlin Street a 'hippy market' takes place nightly).

A religious Jew places Tefillin (Phylacteries or prayer boxes) on a young Israeli.

Off Yoel Salomon Street, on Hillel Street (CU), is **The Time Elevator**, a potted history of the city in high-tech simulator large-film format (closed Saturday). It's well done (if a little expensive) and is a good place for older children. Younger ones may not appreciate the stomach-churning special effects quite so much.

Ben Yehuda Street ends at the busy down-to-earth main thoroughfare of the Jaffa (Yafo) Road, which goes (left) to the Central Bus Station. From here it is a 5-minute walk to Jerusalem's best-quality and liveliest fresh-produce market at **Mahane Yehuda★** (CT). Visit it on Thursday or Friday, before the Sabbath, to catch it in full swing.

The colourful market at Mahane Yehuda.

If you have come to Jerusalem expecting to find old-world, pre-War, shabbily-charming settlements looking like something from *Fiddler on the Roof*, then you will be very disappointed with most of West Jerusalem. Yet there is one surviving *shtetl* (traditional East European Jewish quarter), and that is **Me'a She'arim** (CT), a 5-minute walk north from the Jaffa Road/Ben Yehuda Street junction. Be aware though that this area is not a conventional tourist attraction and certainly no quaint 'heritage village'. Me'a She'arim is the refuge of a community of Ultra-Orthodox hard-line Hasidic Jews, who dress in the traditional garb of mid-18C Eastern Europe (*see* p.19). Visitors are also expected to adhere to a modest dress code, with signs warning visitors (women in particular) to cover up all bare flesh. Men should wear long trousers and women should wear long skirts and long-sleeved tops. Couples should refrain from any show of public affection (no holding hands) and to keep the peace it's best to leave your camera in its case. The main street is Me'a

She'arim Street, and although there are no sights as such, the area is an excellent place to buy Judaica (*see* p.108).

South-west of the Old City, **Yemin Moshé★** (CU) is another pleasant pedestrianised area to explore. One of the first Jewish quarters built outside the Old City in the mid 1800s (through the impetus given by Sir Moses Montefiore, a British philanthropist), it was renovated in the 1970s and is now a highly desirable residential area, popular with artists. A **windmill** constructed in 1857 by Sir Montefiore still stands above the area. From here there are wonderful **views★** over the Old City, especially at night when the ramparts are illuminated.

If you continue further down, you will come to the Hebron Road (Derekh Hevron) (CUV) and see on your left the **Cinematheque**; from the terrace of its restaurant there are also interesting views of the Old City and Mount Zion.

Browsing the bookstalls in the traditional Ultra-Orthodox area of Me'a She'arim.

The Israel Museum★★★

Set in parkland in the affluent suburbs of Western Jerusalem, the Israel Museum (BU) is well deserving of its national museum status. It is most famous as the home of the **Dead Sea Scrolls★★★**, but this aside, there is a mountain of material to look through. The permanent displays are very well presented and temporary exhibitions of international importance are staged throughout the year. Allow at least half a day and preferably a full day here. The museum is a 10-minute ride from the centre on bus nos 9, 17 or 24. It is open daily: Sun, Mon, Wed, Thurs, 10am-5pm; Tues 4pm-10pm (Shrine of the Book 10am-10pm on Tues); Fri 10am-2pm; Sat 10am-4pm.

The Great Isaiah Scroll forms the centrepiece of the Shrine of the Book exhibition.

The museum is divided into seven main sections: Archaeology; the Shrine of the Book, or Dead Sea Scrolls exhibition (*see* p.74); Judaica (Jewish religious objects) and Jewish Ethnography; the Bezalel Art Wing, comprising European art of the last three centuries, Israeli 20C art, plus a worldwide selection; Modern Art and sculpture; Israeli Art (temporary exhibitions); the Youth (children's) Wing.

There are free guided tours, in English, as follows: Museum Highlights, daily (except Sat) 11am, and Tues 4.30pm; Shrine of the

Book, Sun, Mon, Wed, Thurs 1.30pm, Tues 3pm, Fri 12.45pm; Jewish Heritage, Sun and Wed 3pm; Archaeological Treasures, Mon and Thurs 3pm. If you want to go it alone, there are comprehensive illustrated leaflets detailing the highlights of each principal section, or if you are short of time, follow the handy leaflet describing a *Quick Tour of the Museum*, which notionally takes 90 minutes, although it is best to allow 2 hours. The museum web site is www.imj.org.il.

The best strategy is to start with the unmissable **Shrine of the Book**★★★ (in case fatigue takes over later), then take a Museum Highlights tour. Take a break for lunch, and if you have any energy left you can return to those areas of most interest to you. In the **Archaeology** section, the Samuel Bronfman galleries relate the history of the country's first inhabitants through a varied display of interesting finds covering a period of eight millenniums. Among the many other interesting things to do in the **Judaica and Jewish Ethnography** section, do not miss the reconstructed 18C synagogues, especially the Horb Synagogue, from south Germany, with its painted vault, and the Italian synagogue from Vittorio Veneto, with its tripartite Holy Ark, richly decorated with gilded panelling.

Take a break while visiting the different sections of the museum complex, and wander along the **Billy Rose Garden of Art**★, created by the American sculptor and set designer of Japanese origin, Isamu Noguchi. You can see modern sculptures by Rodin (*Balzac*), Zadkine, Henry Moore (*Vertebrae*), Jacques Lipchitz (*Mother and Child*), Vasarely, Picasso (*Profiles*), Germaine Richier, and others.

The Dead Sea Scrolls

What makes the Dead Sea Scrolls so important is that they are the world's oldest biblical manuscripts. And, just as in a Bible tale, they were discovered by accident, by a shepherd boy in a cave looking for his lost flock. The discovery was made at Qumran, on the Dead Sea – hence their name – in 1947.

Initially only seven scrolls were found, yet these turned out to be the most important and complete examples. Over the next nine years, nearly 800 more scrolls and texts, most of them fragmentary, were discovered in nearby caves. Many are written on parchment, mostly in Hebrew, but there are also texts written on papyrus. They had been stored in cylindrical-shaped pottery containers, which in the moisture-free atmosphere of the caves had kept them perfectly preserved. The Scrolls date from the 2C BC until the 1C AD (or 1C CE, meaning 'Common Era', as it is referred to here), and were written by a hermit-like group of monastic Jews called the Essenes, who were wiped out by the Romans.

The meaning of the writings in the Scrolls has been the subject of vigorous debate among historians and scholars ever since they were discovered. Certainly they have

given insights into the formative years of both Christianity and Judaism, even though none of the scrolls contains any explicit mention of Jesus or anyone else in the New Testament. However, it is written in Luke that Jesus read about His messianic calling in the **Great Isaiah Scroll**, which has been dated to His time. Also, other scrolls, such as the **Community Rule** (Manual of Discipline) recall some details of the beginnings of the Jerusalem Church, as mentioned in the New Testament (Acts of the Apostles, Chapter 2). These scrolls, along with the **War Scroll**, the **Temple Scroll** – the longest, at nearly 8.2m (27ft) unfurled – and the **Psalms Scroll**, make up the centrepiece of the Shrine of the Book exhibition.

The striking architecture of the Shrine of the Book is a tribute to the Scrolls. You enter as if into the darkened caves of Qumran, and the main hall is designed in the shape of one of the containers in which the Scrolls were found. The exterior juxtaposition of the gleaming white dome of the Shrine and the adjacent black basalt monolith symbolises the War of the Sons of Light against the Sons of Darkness, as referred to in the War Scroll. Take a guided tour (*see* p.72) to get the most from your visit.

Left: The Shrine of the Book building.
Below: Taking time to decipher the scrolls.

Other Attractions Nearby

Immediately opposite the Israel Museum is the **Bible Lands Museum★★**, which covers events in and beyond Israel (open in summer Sun, Mon, Tues, Thurs 9.30am-5.30pm, Fri 9.30am-2pm, and Wed 9.30am-9.30pm in summer and 1.30-9.30pm in winter). It is quite separate from the Israel Museum but in terms of archaeology and history there are inevitably areas which overlap. It is a fine museum, very modern, well laid out and with some excellent exhibits. In any other location, it would be an important attraction; here it suffers by comparison. You won't have the energy or time to do both the Israel Museum and this one in a day, but you might well wish to spend a day and a half at the former and a half day here.

In the same parkland as the two museums is the **Knesset** (BU), Israel's parliament, a featureless modern building. Outside stands a huge much-photographed *menorah*, the

The menorah outside the Knesset, a gift from the British Parliament, shows scenes from Jewish history.

Judaic seven-branched candelabra that is the symbol of the State of Israel. Inside, the most famous feature is the vibrant **Chagall Tapestries★**, painted by the famous Russian-born Jewish artist, Marc Chagall. Entry is free, by guided tour only (Sun-Thurs 8.30am-2.30pm), but you will need your passport to gain admission.

A 10-minute walk away is the little-visited **Monastery of the Cross** (BU), a striking building founded in the 11C on the site of the tree which was used for the True Cross. Some 400 monks once lived here, but today it is largely empty. The present Superior will take you on a guided tour (daily 10am-1.30pm), which includes 17C frescoes and 5C mosaics.

Yad VaShem★★★

Some 2.5km (1.5 miles) to the west of the Israel Museum lies **Yad VaShem★★★** (AU), Israel's national memorial to the Holocaust. Its name is taken from the Bible (*Isaiah 56:5*) and means 'a memorial and a name' (that will not perish). All Israeli school-children, and most visiting heads of state, are brought to visit this most fearful of all exhibitions (open Sun-Fri; admission free). Numerous buses go from the centre of town, including nos 13, 16, 17, 18, 20, 21, 23, 24, 26, 27, 39 and 99 – the latter provides a sightseeing tour of Jerusalem, finishing up at Yad VaShem.

The main exhibition, the **Historical Museum**, chronicles the Holocaust of 1939-45 in graphic detail, using large black-and-white photographs, artefacts and short films. It is very well presented with clear, informative, largely dispassionate text, but its distressing images will haunt you long

The unforgettably poignant Children's Memorial, Yad VaShem.

after you have left Yad VaShem. Particular attention is drawn to the fate of children, who made up one in four of the six million or so Holocaust victims. The **Children's Memorial**, a darkened, atmospheric multi-mirrored hall, with flickering candles receding into infinity to indicate the 1.5 million souls lost, is intensely poignant. In **The Valley of the Communities**, the names of some 5 000 Jewish communities that disappeared in the Holocaust are carved into huge blocks of stone, the bedrock of Israel. The Eternal Flame, in the **Hall of Remembrance**, surrounded by names of concentration camps engraved on the floor, is another dramatic representation. Other areas include a **Hall of Names**, research centres and an art gallery.

Ein Kerem★★

The picturesque village of **Ein Kerem★★** ('En Kerem) is set in a valley surrounded by olive trees and terraced vineyards, about 7km

(4.5 miles) south-west of Jerusalem. Though increasingly threatened by urban sprawl from the New City, this quiet settlement nestling among the trees offers a refreshing break from the bustle of the city. It is thought to be the birthplace of John the Baptist. Today, its lovely old stone houses are home to artists, several galleries and some good restaurants.

The Franciscan **Church of St John** dates from the late 17C, though it is built over older remains. Remnants of Byzantine mosaics can be seen through a grille, and steps lead down to the grotto where St John was said to have been born.

On a street to the left of the main road, a second Franciscan church, the **Church of the Visitation**, is reputed to be built on the site of the house of St John's parents, Zacharias and Elizabeth, who were visited here by the Virgin Mary. The Byzantines worshipped in a natural grotto on the site, and later the Crusaders built a two-storied church over the grotto. The Crusader church was destroyed after they left, but in 1862 the Franciscans restored the Lower Church, which is adorned with large **frescoes**. The Upper Church was built in 1955 by the **Italian Antonio Barluzzi** – look for the apse of the Crusader church.

On the hill above Ein Kerem (walkers with sturdy shoes can take the rather rough path from the Church of the Visitation) is the new **Hadassah Medical Centre** (Giryat Hadassah), built in the 1950s to replace the previous centre on Mount Scopus. It is famous for the stunning **Chagall windows★★**. The 12 stained-glass windows in the synagogue to the left of the main entrance feature each of the tribes of Israel.

EXCURSIONS

📖 Bethlehem

Bethlehem (Bet Lehem, or Beit Lahm in
Arabic), the birthplace of Jesus, lies just
10km (6 miles) south of Jerusalem, and these
days is almost a suburb. It's best to forget all
those romantic Christmas carols and
children's storybook images – today's town is
a prosaic, dusty, traffic-snarled place. Millions
of dollars were pumped into here for the
Millennium celebrations, though, in the
short term at least, all the building work has
made things worse than ever. Hopefully, the
near future will see Bethlehem reap the

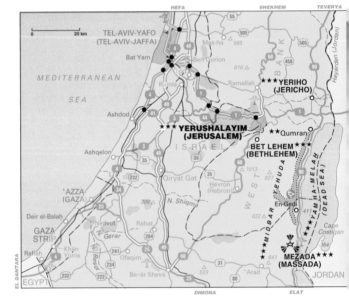

Note: The West Bank and Gaza Strip are territories under provisional status.

Rachel's Tomb, Bethlehem, is much visited by Jewish women praying for fertility or a safe birth.

rewards of this investment.

Bethlehem is in fact part of the Palestinian-controlled West Bank, and en route you pass through a checkpoint, which for a tourist should pose no problems. By contrast, Palestinians wishing to go the other way, to work each day in Jerusalem, may do so only on foot because of the Israeli fear of car bombs – hence the huge number of cars parked at the roadside.

Just outside the entrance to Bethlehem is **Rachel's Tomb**, a place revered by Muslims, Christians and Jews. Rachel was the wife of Jacob and died here giving birth to Benjamin. The velvet-covered tomb is the only object in a very plain room.

The hub of activity in Bethlehem is **Manger Square**, where coaches disgorge pilgrims to be accosted by souvenir-sellers and guides. On the square, the **Church of the Nativity** is one of the oldest place of pilgrimage in all Christendom. It was proclaimed as the birthplace of Christ by St Helena (mother of the Emperor Constantine), and consecrated in 339. Her original church was mostly rebuilt by the Emperor Justinian in the 6C but, unlike almost every other significant church in the Holy Land, it has escaped destruction since then and so is one of the oldest Christian churches in the world.

The unusual low entrance at the front door is a Crusader amendment, designed to stop attackers on horseback entering the church, so it is said. This is the original 6C church, quite atmospheric, if a little frayed at the edges, and suffering (like the Church of the Holy Sepulchre) from being managed and bickered over by different denominations – Roman Catholics, Greek Orthodox and Armenians – who share no brotherly love. In 1984 the latter two literally came to blows over a territorial dispute inside the church.

Look for the ancient **mosaic panels** beneath the wooden trapdoors and on the side walls to get an idea of how fine the original Byzantine church might have looked. The birthplace is below the church, in the **Grotto of the Nativity**, reached by steps to the right of the altar – there may well be a long queue to get in. The supposed actual place of the

The supposed actual place of the birth of Jesus, in the Grotto of the Nativity, Bethlehem.

birth is marked by a 14-point vermeil (silver-gilt) star, and opposite is a stone manger where the baby was laid. Even these simple symbols cause major divisions. Each of the three denominations have replaced the others' silver star, and the last dispute, in

1853, is even cited as one of the reasons for the Crimean War! Meanwhile, the 'real' manger has been removed to the church of Santa Maria Maggiore, in Rome.

Built onto the Church of the Nativity is the **Church of St Catherine**, a modern soulless accretion finished in 1881, from where the Christmas Eve midnight mass is televised each year.

Off Manger Square leads **Milk Grotto Street**, named after a cave halfway along here in which the Virgin is said to have taken refuge on the flight of the Holy Family to Egypt. Milk from her breast dripped on the floor and turned the cavern from red to a milky white. It is claimed that eating a little of this rock will cure women of infertility and improve lactation, and as you will see handfuls have been gouged out. That practice has now been stopped by the church – instead a monk sells bags of rock deposits to despairing infertile pilgrims!

The Grotto of the Nativity, Bethlehem.

The Dead Sea★★★

Nestling in a depression at 400m (1 312ft) below sea-level, the Dead Sea (Yam Ha-Melah) is the lowest place on earth. And it is this very fact that causes the sterility of its water. The Dead Sea (which is actually a lake measuring 77km/49 miles by 10km/6 miles) is fed by the River Jordan and flash floods but with nowhere lower to flow out to, it simply evaporates in the scorching heat. This means that its mineral content is concentrated to an astonishing 30 per cent solids (normal sea water is around 4 per cent solids), and the only life that can survive in its viscous waters are a few hardy bacteria. Eventually, on the edges of the sea, particularly in the southern half, the water evaporates completely, leaving behind glistening white mineral deposits which are eagerly harvested by mining companies.

Slap it on and feel the benefit – enjoying the mud at Ein Gedi spa.

In a clever stroke of marketing, new life, in the form of tourism, is being breathed into this parched, inhospitable region by its promotion as a spa resort and a variety of treatments are on offer. On a less serious health kick, coachloads of holidaymakers visit daily to slap black rejuvenating mud all over themselves, before floating in the Dead Sea. It's a sight and experience you should not miss, but you must also beware of the potential pitfalls of this hostile environment.

If you have the slightest cut on your body (men, don't

The secret of bathing in the Dead Sea is to relax, sit back, as if sinking into your favourite armchair, then slowly stretch out. Even this seemingly simple manoeuvre takes a little getting used to, as the extra buoyancy of the water can flip you over like a rubber duck! Be careful, as it is no joke if you get the water in your eyes or mouth.

shave that morning!) the Dead Sea salts will find it. The discomfort is double for getting water in your eyes (akin to hot gravel), or mouth (a truly sickening sensation). For women, bathing during a period should be avoided. Swimming in the conventional sense is out of the question, and splashing is just about the most heinous crime imaginable here. The thing to do, as probably everyone knows from the pictures, is to lie back, stretch out and read the *Jerusalem Post*. After your bathing session you'll need a shower to wash the minerals off your body, and particularly from your hair, both of which will be covered in a sticky, oily film.

There are three designated bathing areas, with lifeguards and showers. The most popular, and nearest to Jerusalem, is at **Ein Gedi** ('En Gedi, pronounced *en-geddy*). Beware while swimming, as thieves come here, too. If you are not on a tour coach, there are around ten Egged buses a day from Jerusalem (nos 421, 444, 486), which take about 90 minutes to get here.

Ein Gedi is also famous for its oasis-like **nature reserve★**, set between two canyons, with waterfalls, a spring and a number of marked hiking trails (closed Friday). Avoid holidays and weekends as it gets very busy. If you can get here first thing in the morning, it is well worth the effort to beat the crowds.

The best time to visit the Dead Sea is in winter, or at least outside summer when the temperature regularly rises above 40°C and the place becomes one huge sauna.

The cheapest and quickest way to visit the Dead Sea is to take one of the 12-hour tours on offer. These depart from the city in the small hours, at 3 to 3.30am, arriving at

Masada★★★ (see below) just in time to climb
to the summit to witness the spectacular
sunrise. They then go on to Ein Gedi, where
there is time for a quick dip in the Dead Sea,
followed by brief stops at **Qumran★★** (where
the Dead Sea Scrolls were discovered) and
Jericho (Yeriho, or Arīhā in Arabic – visit the
excavations of ancient biblical Jericho at **Tel
Es-Sultān**, and **Kirbet El Mefjer★**, the ruins
of the 6C palace of a caliph named Hisham),
before returning to Jerusalem. The clientele
on this tour are mostly backpackers – you'll
find details circulated in most hostels. If the
idea of getting up so early does not appeal,
there is a tour that leaves at 9am and returns
at 5pm. It includes a visit to Masada, a mud
bath at Ein Gedi, a swim in the Dead Sea and
lunch at the snack bar there. The Tourist
Information Centre will book this tour for
you or you can book a guided tour direct at
United Tours, 9 Coresh Street, next to Zahal
Square (CU), ☎ **02 625 2187/8** (*see also* p.124).

A word of warning: To avoid dehydration
on a trip to the Dead Sea area you should
drink plenty of water (half a litre per hour is
recommended).

*This aerial view of
Masada shows its
spectacular
plateau-top location
– a daunting
challenge for any
invaders, though not
impossible for the
Romans.*

Masada★★★

The very name Masada (Massada, literally
'fortress') is a clarion call to an Israeli –
death or glory, no surrender. All Israeli
schoolchildren are brought to Masada, and
armed forces personnel are sworn in here
with the words 'Masada shall not fall again!'

It is without doubt a dramatic place, an
island of almost sheer cliff, rising 440m
(1 443ft) above the Dead Sea. Its top is
flattened into a plateau measuring 650m by
300m (2 133ft by 984ft), a perfect location
for a desert stronghold and taken advantage

of by the Maccabees between 103 and 76 BC.

Some 30 years later, Herod the Great acquired Masada. He kept it as a contingency, to be used to escape from the rebellious Jews of Jerusalem, but, being Herod the Great, he still demanded creature comforts so he ordered the construction of a splendid palace. Thoughtfully, he had huge water cisterns and great grain stores built, capable of withstanding a siege of many years. Herod died in AD 4, without ever having need to use his bolthole, so it was with no little irony that in AD 66 a militant group of Jews called the Zealots captured Masada and settled on top, thumbing their noses at the Romans below, while taking full advantage of their erstwhile enemy's foresight. Unable to dislodge the Zealot community by a conventional assault, and busy on other fronts, the Romans left them alone for several years. In AD 72 they returned, and camped below Masada with a force of 15 000 men. The defenders, by now almost 1 000 strong, watched in horror as an army of slaves were set to work constructing a giant ramp of earth and rock, which was to stretch from the nearest hillside right up to their main gate. As it neared completion, they knew that butchery and rape, or at the very least a lifetime of slavery, was the fate in store for every man, woman and child.

In order to spare themselves this degradation and to cheat the Romans of a great propaganda victory, they decided on mass suicide. It was the duty of each man to kill his wife and children, then ten men were chosen by lots to execute the others. When these ten had finished their grisly duty, one man would kill the other nine, set Masada on fire, then fall onto his own sword. It is

Climb Masada at sunrise and listen to the story of the siege on top of the great rock itself, while gazing down at the Roman earth ramp and imagining the fear of the defenders.

said that they did not set fire to the warehouses where they kept their stock of food, to prove that they did not kill themselves because they were starving. When the Romans entered the burning city they found 960 bodies; the only survivors were two women and five children who had hidden to escape the slaughter. The story was related by them to the famous Roman historian, Josephus, who recounted it in his authoritative chronicle *The Jewish War*.

Monks occupied the site during the 4C and 5C but after that Masada was deserted, and indeed almost completely forgotten until its rediscovery in the mid 19C.

The classic way to visit the site is to walk up to the fortress, arriving at the top as the sun rises; special Dead Sea tours enable you to do this (*see* p.86). The walk takes from 30 to 60 minutes, depending on your level of fitness. If all this sounds a bit daunting you can always take the cable-car instead – though this service does not start until 8am. At the other end of the day, there is a son et lumière performance (*see* p.104).

There's enough left of Herod's great palace to give you a good idea of the scale and grandeur of Masada, but a visit here is more about the **views***** of the surrounding **Judean Desert***** and the Dead Sea, the spectacle of the site and the atmosphere of hearing the legend in situ, rather than an archaeological tour. Even the most sceptical will find it a moving experience.

The remarkable Judean Desert landscape can be viewed from the middle terrace of the Northern Palace, Masada.

THE SPIRIT OF JERUSALEM

Jerusalem is perhaps the most intriguing, fascinating, yet perplexing and bewildering tourist city in the world. Nowhere else comes with such great expectations heaped upon its shoulders; like Jesus, it struggles with this Cross, and like Him, it sometimes fails.

Paradoxically, although it is the world's leading Christian pilgrimage destination it is not an easy or spiritually comfortable place, and pilgrims who come seeking answers may well depart with more questions of their own. Why do priests of the same religion come to blows over ownership of a meaningless wooden beam in a church? Why are there two tombs of Mary, two tombs of Jesus and three places of the Ascension? And who is this strange fellow in fancy dress at the city gate who thinks he is King David? Well, actually his name is Bruce, he is from Australia and he is a perfect example of Jerusalem Syndrome. This is not a myth but a well-documented clinical condition which occurs when visitors become so overpowered by the religious atmosphere of the city that they take on the personality of a biblical

An Israeli soldier talks with Ultra-Orthodox Jews on Ben Yehuda Street.

character and choose to stay on here.

In fact, little is what it seems to be in Jerusalem, as much with its custodians as with its more eccentric long-term guests. Far from being a city of brotherly love, at times intolerance crackles in the divided air. Yet the essential paradox of Jerusalem is that despite the differences the visitor can detect a hint of hope for greater tolerance and harmony in this divided city.

For the dispassionate observer, however, all this activity and confusion is grist to the mill, a frisson in the air. It's rather wonderful to be personally greeted at the gate of Jerusalem by a biblical lyre-plucking king. And two tombs *are* more interesting than one. But most importantly, you soon learn that Jerusalem is not the sort of city where you tick off sites on a cultural, archaeological or religious trawl; rather than being presented with mere solutions, here you have thought-provoking alternatives. It is your Jerusalem: make of it what you will.

Jerusalem is not the sort of place for typical holiday reading. It is often said that the finest guide book to the Holy Land is the Bible, with many references to the city, both in the Old and New Testaments. If you find the language of the classical King James Authorised Version off-putting, there are modern translations that make things easier, or try *The Jerusalem that Jesus Knew*, by John Wilkinson. *Jerusalem*, by the travel writer Colin Thubron, is a short atmospheric browse through Jerusalem, with reflections on several aspects of the city. In a similar vein is *Jerusalem: City of Mirrors*, by the Israeli writer Amos Elon. *The Mandelbaum Gate*, by Muriel Spark, is an acclaimed novel of love and espionage set against the divided Jerusalem of the 1960s. On the broader theme of the struggle for nationhood and the events immediately after the Second World War is the classic *Exodus*, by Leon Uris.

WEATHER

Jerusalem enjoys hot dry summers and endures cold wet winters. Temperatures are rarely too extreme, however, with an average maximum of around 30°C and a low of 11°C, so at any time of year it's rarely uncomfortable. The city's altitude means that it's several degrees cooler than the searing heat of the adjacent Judean Desert, and its low humidity makes the hot summer days

The Dome of the Rock, during a brief winter snowfall.

more bearable. In the winter months (November-March) a brief flurry of snow has been known, and the winds can be chill, but between the rainfalls there are also some gloriously clear, crisp, sunny days. And it's easy to beat the winter blues. Just hop on a Dead Sea bus and in 90 minutes you are back to 25°C.

The high altitude also means that at most times of year you will need a light jumper for the evenings, and outside summer (October-April) you should be prepared for rain. The best time to visit, weather-wise, is May or September.

CALENDAR OF EVENTS

The following are events and festivals of a secular nature. For religious events *see* p. 120. To confirm the dates of the events below and for all other one-off events, ask the tourist office for a copy of *Israel Events*.

Late May-mid June: Israel Festival, a three-week celebration with performing arts from all over the world.

June-July: International Film Festival at Jerusalem Cinematheque.

July: International Folklore Festival – an arts and craft fair, including music and folklore.

August: International Festival of Puppet Theatre.

ACCOMMODATION

Jerusalem has been accommodating visitors for nearly 1 700 years, and not surprisingly has a good number of places to stay. Avoid the main religious holidays of Christmas and Easter and you should be able to find room at the inn. High season is July and August.

The principal choices are modern, mid- to high-priced international-style **hotels** in West Jerusalem; good value hotels offering a reasonable range of facilities but indifferent locations in East Jerusalem; and older, more characterful inexpensive hotels or budget **hostels**. Hostels are used typically either by backpackers, or by religious groups, and can be found either in the Old City, in East Jerusalem or attached to religious institutions. Although you do not have to be a Christian to stay at the Christian-run hostels, note that many operate a curfew. While staying in the Old City is convenient for the sights and is certainly atmospheric during the day, it closes down at night and its narrow, often poorly-lit streets and alleys can be daunting. East Jerusalem may be a better bet, and is within easy walking distance of the Old City.

Hostels are not graded but vary in degrees of comfort, from spartan to about the equivalent of a 3-star hotel. There are currently five officially affiliated **Hostels International (HI)** in Jerusalem, details of which can be obtained from the Israeli Youth Hostel Association, International Convention Centre, PO Box 6001, Jerusalem Z.C. 91060 ☎ **02 655 8400**, Fax 02 655 8430, e-mail: iyha@iyha.org.il, web site www.youth-hostels. org.il.

Fully fledged 4- and 5-star hotels are generally quite expensive, almost on a par with European capitals. The **Israeli Hotel Association** (☎ **03 517 0131** Fax 03 510 0197) has an up-to-date list of hotels and prices on its web site www.israel-hotels.org.il.

Hotel rooms are priced in US dollars and this is how you should pay your bill, to avoid the addition of 17% VAT. The following prices are a guide to what you can expect to pay for a double room in a central hotel, per night, usually with breakfast included (but do check first). Note that special deals and discounts (always ask) can reduce these rates dramatically.

Expensive	$150-250
Moderate	$100-150
Inexpensive	$60-100
Budget	less than $60

Recommendations

Expensive

King David 23 King David Street (David Ha-Malek) (CU) ☎ 02 620 8888 Fax 02 620 8882 (or toll-free from the UK 0800 731 2789)
e-mail: danhtls@danhotels.co.il
If you want to rub shoulders with royalty and statesmen, this is still the place to be. It may have lost a little of its sheen in recent years but the King David is still *the* Jerusalem address.

Hilton Jerusalem 7 King David Street ☎ 02 621 2121 Fax 02 621 1000 (international toll-free Europe 00 800 444 58667)
e-mail: jrshitwrm@hilton.com
Like the King David further along the street, it faces the Old City and has good views, especially from the terrace. With outdoor pool and large shopping arcade. Room prices vary according to whether the view is of the Old or New City.

Expensive/Moderate

American Colony Nablus Road (Derekh Shekhem) (DT) ☎ 02 627 9777 Fax 02 627 9779 (or toll-free from the UK 0800 960 239, from USA 212 8560115)
e-mail: reserve@amcol.co.il
Jerusalem's most atmospheric and stylish old-world hotel (*see* p.56), ideally placed in a quiet spot a short walk from the Old City. The cheaper rooms are the best value.

Mount Zion Hotel 17 Hebron Road (Derekh Hevron) (CU) ☎ 02 568 9555 Fax 02 673 1425 e-mail: hotel@mountzion.co.il
Comfortable brand new hotel, in a good position some 10-15 minutes' walk from both the Old City and the New City centre. Nice grounds and a swimming pool.

Novotel Jerusalem 9 St George Street (DT) ☎ 02 500 8500 Fax 02 500 2121
A new hotel opened this year, in the same area as the American Colony hotel, just a ten-minute walk from Damascus Gate. 390 rooms, outdoor pool, main restaurant serving buffet meals, local and international cuisine.

Hanagid Hotel 7 Schatz Street ☎ 02 622 1111 Fax 02 624 8420
This Best Western hotel is one of the few hotels situated in the centre of the New City, just a few minutes away from the Ben Yehuda mall and Zion Square, where most of the restaurants and bars are.

YMCA Three Arches 26 King David Street ☎ 02 569 2692 Fax 02 623 5192 e-mail: y3arches@netvision.net.il
Often described, probably quite justifiably, as the world's nicest YMCA (definitely not your usual YMCA crowd!), this is a semi-luxury hotel by any other

name, occupying an imposing landmark Art Deco tower opposite the exclusive King David hotel. Good restaurant, fitness centre and a swimming pool (*see* p.96).

Moderate

Christ Church Guest House *PO Box 14037, Jaffa Gate, Old City* (FY) ☎ 02 627 7727 Fax 02 628 2999 e-mail: christch@netvision.net.il Situated at the Jaffa Gate, right on the edge of the Old City, opposite David's Tower. Enjoys a pleasant and quiet setting: pretty courtyard and garden, comfortable bedrooms, private parking. Breakfast buffet and Friday Night Shabbat Meal. But – no-smoking throughout,

unmarried couples not allowed to share a room, and curfew at 11pm.

Inexpensive

St George's Cathedral Pilgrim Guest House *20 Nablus Road, (entrance to Cathedral)* (DT) ☎ 02 628 3302 Fax 02 628 2253 e-mail: sghotel@netvision.net.il Peace and quiet in the lovely historic setting of the grounds of St George's Cathedral, less than a 10-minute walk from the Damascus Gate. Nice rooms set around a courtyard garden. Friendly and relaxed atmosphere (no 'religious pressure'). Breakfast buffet.
Jerusalem Hotel *Nablus Road* ☎ 02 628 3282 Fax 02 627 1356

The modern Mount Zion Hotel is built into the hillside.

(or toll-free from UK 0800 328 2393, or from USA 1 800 657 9401)

e-mail: raed@jrshotel.com

Apart from the fact that it is situated just in front of the Arab central bus station, its location near Damascus Gate makes it easy to visit the Old City. The building itself has a beautiful façade, with a pleasant court-yard for outside dining.

Armenian Patriarchate Guest House *Via Dolorosa, near the junction with El-Wäd Road* (FX) ☎ 02 626 0880 Fax 02 626 1208

The YMCA Three Arches Hotel.

Situated in the Old City, in the Muslim Quarter, its rooms and bathrooms are clean and recently renovated. No break-fast available at present as renovation is still in progress. Very quiet at night, but a rude awakening thanks to the muezzin!

YMCA Capitolina *29 Nablus Road* (DT) ☎ 02 628 6888 Fax 02 627 6301

Jerusalem's other YMCA, set in the less fashionable Eastern part of the city, is not a patch on the architecture or status of its swankier Western sister. But it is much cheaper and, with comfortable rooms and excellent free sports/health club facilities, offers very good value. Good quiet location, close to the American Colony, just a short walk from the Old City.

Inexpensive/Budget

Jerusalem Inn Hotel *7 Horkenos Street* (CU) ☎ 02 625 2757 Fax 02 625 1297

e-mail: jerinn@netvision.net.il

Right at the heart of the West Jerusalem action, near Zion Square, this is a popular, well-run modern place, which is very good value for money. The downstairs Café offers assorted copious breakfasts and inexpensive homemade lunch specials.

FOOD AND DRINK

The food of Jerusalem is, like the city, mostly a tale of East and West. The former is Arabic or Middle Eastern, the latter is cosmopolitan – French, Italian, Mediterranean are popular themes but, surprisingly, traditional Jewish cuisine is not common. As in most major world cities, there are also numerous styles of restaurant serving virtually all kinds of international food.

Although eating out in Jerusalem is nearly always pleasurable, by Western holiday resort standards it is expensive. Remember too that the service charge of 10-15% (*see* p.122) is nearly always additional. To cut costs, look for special deals at lunchtime which even many top restaurants offer.

Jewish and Western-style restaurants

The main characteristic of non-Arabic restaurants in Jerusalem is the practice of **kosher** cooking. This is a ritualised preparation of food, the best-known instruction of which involves the complete separation of dairy products and meat. Steaks in cream sauce, cheeseburgers and the like are, therefore, forbidden. Pork (regarded as unclean) and shellfish are also proscribed.

Most, but not all, restaurants in West Jerusalem are kosher and respect the Sabbath, closing late on Friday afternoon and re-opening on Saturday evening.

The good news for vegetarians is that the kosher injunction has led to the development of **dairy** restaurants or cafés, which specialise in salads, soups, pies, quiches and pizzas. Many of these are also known as dairy and fish restaurants, invariably serving sole, salmon, trout, perhaps bream and tuna, and usually **St Peter's Fish** – a

Popular street food – spit-grilled shwarma (kebab).

97

freshwater tilapia from the Sea of Galilee, which can be delicious.

Middle Eastern restaurants

Meat-lovers will have a field day at most Middle Eastern restaurants, where there is usually a mouth-watering selection of high-quality kebabs and grilled meats. Start your meal off with the *mezze* (literally a 'mix' or assortment), which gives you a taste of several appetisers. Lebanese, Persian and Moroccan eating houses add an exotic spice to the city's culinary mix.

Street food

The two staple street foods of Jerusalem (in fact, all Israel) are **humus** and **falafel**, enjoyed equally by Israelis and Palestinians. Both dishes derive from the humble chick pea: *humus* is a creamy puréed dip, *falafel* is crushed chick peas, flavoured with spices and herbs, rolled into balls which are covered in a crisp, crumbed coating and deep-fried. Both are served with freshly cooked pitta bread. *Falafel* is generally stuffed into a pitta pocket with a large choice of help-yourself sauces, salads and pickles.

The third common street food is **shwarma** (or shawarma). Like doner kebab, this is pressed meat (usually lamb) sliced off a vertically rotating spit. It is served, like *falafel*, in a pitta pocket, with optional chilli tomato sauce. *Shwarma* and *falafel* are most common as takeaway foods, but there are also a number of basic sit-down cafés, particularly in the Old City, which specialise in these snacks. Those in the Muslim Quarter are renowned for their *humus* and may serve only this, sometimes accompanied by a tasty dark-brown mashed bean dish from Egypt, known as *fuul* (pronounced *fool*). Look in the Old City's Souq Khan ez-Zeit for *shwarma* sellers.

Fresh humus is a favourite snack.

Another great place for carnivores, as long as you are not too squeamish, is the Mahane Yehuda market (*see* p.69). Street vendors here specialise in that hotchpotch of beef, onions, spices and assorted offal served in pitta, known as *meorav Yerushalmi* – Jerusalem meats.

Bagels, surprisingly, are not as big here as in Jewish enclaves in the Western world. Devotees also point out that, in their opinion, they are not as good in Jerusalem as in places like London or New York. Here, they are steamed before baking, whereas in the West they are usually boiled – so expect a crisper, drier texture.

Finally, if you are passing a Jewish bakery in the morning, pop in for a fresh *bureka*, a small pastry filled with either spinach, cheese or potatoes.

Alcoholic drinks

There is no beer-drinking culture in Jerusalem in the same way as in the West. Muslims do not drink alcohol, so it's soft drinks only in most Arab-owned establishments (the more touristy ones may be licensed). There are 'pubs' and bars, mostly along and off Yoel Salomon Street, catering for trendy young locals and tourists, but drinks are expensive so you may wish to follow the local example and drink very slowly! Alternatively, look out for 'happy hours'.

Israeli wines have improved a lot in recent years and are worth trying. Many of these are produced to kosher specifications.

Tea and coffee

Apart from speciality outlets, both tea and coffee are generally of poor quality, and if you are in a kosher restaurant serving meat dishes, you won't be served milk (a soya-milk substitute may be available). If you crave a good cuppa, look out for one of the newer places around Zion Square in the pedestrianised quarter, where an outdoor café culture has recently emerged. Watch out for the 'Israeli cappuccino', however, which is a mountain of whipped cream and little else!

Tea and coffee in Arabic establishments is always small, black and usually brewed with sugar which makes it very sweet. Ask for it without sugar, then you can add to taste. It's the custom of some places to flavour the coffee with cardamom.

Recommendations

Here is a selection of places which capture the spirit of eating, and, to a lesser degree, drinking in Jerusalem. Dining in these places is moderately priced, except where indicated. Telephone numbers are given only where reservations are recommended.

You should also pick up *Jerusalem Menus*, a useful free listings booklet of 75 of the city's better places to eat. Your hotel will probably have a copy or you can check it out on the web: www.jerusalem-menus.co.il

Restaurants

American Colony *Nablus Road* (DT) ☎ 02 627 9777
Offers a choice of restaurants, most of which are very atmospheric as befits this venerable ex-Pasha's palace (*see* p.56). A light lunch in its courtyard can be heavenly, though the food, and in particular the service, in its more formal and expensive restaurant areas can be variable.

Armenian Tavern *79 Armenian Patriarchate Road* (EZ)
☎ 02 627 3854
It's not every day you will get the chance to try Armenian cuisine, and the Old City setting – the basement of a 12C church, with beautiful tiles and a fountain courtyard – is enchanting. The *khoghoghi derev*, spiced minced meat in vine leaves, comes highly recommended (closed Monday).

Nafoura *18 Latin Patriarchate Street* ☎ 02 626 0034
In the Old City, at the foot of the ramparts near Jaffa Gate. Grilled meat dishes, mezzes and salads can be enjoyed in the shaded courtyard topped by the ramparts.

Le Tsriff *5 Horkenos Street* (CU)
☎ 02 625 5488
Peaceful atmosphere and comfortable setting in this old house where the French cuisine main dishes are good, though pricey. Fresh homemade bread, large choice of wines and attentive staff. An address to keep in mind especially on a Shabbat evening when many places are closed!

Yemenite Step *10 Yoel Moshe Salomon Street*
A city legend, the Yemenite Step may be full of tourists but is still well worth a visit. The speciality is *malawah*, a great fluffy pastry bread, stuffed with sweet or savoury fillings, some of which are spicy Yemenite specialities.

Cacao *Jerusalem Cinematheque, 1 Hebron Road (Derekh Hevron)* (CU) ☎ 02 671 0632
This stylish Mediterranean-style dairy and fish restaurant is part of the trendy Cinematheque complex. Cooking is high-quality and inventive, with prices slightly above average. An outdoor terrace offers fine views of the Old City (open

daily 10am-3am; live jazz Friday 5-9pm; classical string quartet every other Saturday 11am-2pm).

Stanley's *3 Horkenos Street*
☎ 02 625 9459

A superb combination of meaty South African treats and more delicate French cuisine, served up in one of Jerusalem's oldest houses. The service is exemplary. Expensive in the evening but one of the best-value lunches in town.

Philadelphia *Al-Zahra Street (free shuttle service from your hotel)*
☎ 02 628 9770

One of the best-known Arabic and Middle Eastern restaurants in Jerusalem, the Philadelphia has been trading for over 30 years, largely on the quality of its *mezze* and grilled meats.

Café-restaurants

Abu Shukri *63 El-Wād Road* (FX)
This is *the* place, so it is said, for *humus*. It's basic, quite friendly and the *humus* is, indeed, very good, though unless you are an expert you will probably enjoy it no less at one of the neighbouring joints on the El-Wād Road.

Tmol Shilshom *5 Yoel Salomon Street (entrance at the back)* (CU)
A charming place for book-lovers and vegetarians, this café-restaurant-cum-bookshop is set in a cosy traditional Jerusalem stone house. Creative dairy and fish cuisine can be enjoyed while listening to book readings, jazz and folk music. Open until 2am.

Little Jerusalem (Ticho House) *9 Harav Kook Street, off Zion Square* (CU)
A cultural centre and small museum set in a 19C Jerusalem golden-stone house, the Ticho House is worth a visit at any time of the day. Breakfasts, plus dairy and fish cuisine, are served from 10am onwards. Various musical events are regularly staged (see *Jerusalem Menus* for details). This is also one of the few places in the city to offer a specially priced children's menu.

Bars

Fink's *2 Ha-Histadrut Street (corner of King George V Street)* (CU) ☎ 02 623 4523
A Jerusalem institution, best known as the city's oldest and most famous bar but also serving hearty East European Jewish cooking (expensive – and small, so book ahead).

Tzuff *Hebron Road (next to Mount Zion Hotel)* (CU)
Set in a historic old house, with views onto the Old City walls, this is one of the trendiest music bars in town. The crowd are young and good-looking, and the music gets louder as the night wears on.

ENTERTAINMENT AND NIGHTLIFE

There is a rumour gleefully circulated in Tel Aviv that after dark Jerusalem is closed for business. However, a stroll down the Midrahov, the pedestrianised area of the New City, on a Thursday or Saturday night should dispel that myth for ever. In fact, at peak times here it is impossible to stroll – you are simply swept along by the tide. Yet while there is certainly a buzz in the New City, in most of the city things are quiet, with the Old City and East Jerusalem more or less shutting down at nightfall. There is no pub or bar culture (which is not to say there are no pubs or bars), and nightspots are at a premium for fear of disturbing the city's inherently conservative rules and regulations.

For all events, highbrow or lowbrow, check the Friday listing section of the *Jerusalem Post*.

Bars, cafés and clubs

For the best and liveliest bars and cafés, head for the New City, especially along Yoel Salomon Street and Rivlin Street, in the Midrahov (CU). Here the city's bright young things are as well turned out as

Relaxing with friends in the Trio Café, Yoel Salomon Street.

in most European capitals, and eat and drink right through the night until as late as 3am (Fridays excluded). The most pub-like of them all is the prosaically named **Tavern**, on Rivlin Street, which claims to be Jerusalem's oldest pub. The trendy new café alley is Rehov Aza – check out **Filter**, **Moment** and **Atara** – if you can get in through the crowds!

The most popular, indeed the only nightclub in this part of the city, is the cheap and rowdy **Underground**, on Yoel Salomon Street. You may enjoy it if you're under 25 and not too fussy. If you want a better class of rave, you'll have to take a *sherut* (shared taxi) either to the industrial suburb of Talpiot (Talpiyyot), where there is a handful of clubs, or better still, on to Tel Aviv (45-60 minutes away). **Haoman 17** was apparently *the* place to go in Talpiot, but it's best to take local advice as to where's hot and where's not at the time of your visit, as the scene changes so rapidly.

Another much smaller night-life enclave, which is frequented more by travellers and locals than by mainstream tourists, is the Russian Compound, a short stroll from the Midrahov, back towards the Old City, just off the Jaffa Road. The most popular places are centred on Heleni Ha-Malka Street and Monbaz Street (CU). **Glasnost** is the place to go for live music, while **Kanabis** (in name only) and **Strudel**, an internet café, are other fashionable hang-outs.

Folklore and theatre

To enjoy a rare example of Jewish-Palestinian cooperation and a thoroughly entertaining night of song and dance, go to one of the 2-hour folklore shows staged at the **YMCA Auditorium**, King David Street (nightly at 9pm, except Friday and Sunday). A Jewish troupe provides that Yiddish *Fiddler on the Roof* atmosphere, while their Palestinian counterparts perform various Arab dances.

Most theatrical performances are in Hebrew only. The main exception is the **JEST** (Jerusalem English-Speaking Theatre), based at the **Gerard Behar Theatre**, 11 Bezalel ☎ 02 625 1139 (CU). Look on their web site for what's coming: www.geocities.com/Broadway/1824.

Films

Arthouse and classic films are screened nightly at the **Cinematheque**, Hebron Road ☎ 02 672 4143 (which also has a fine café-restaurant, *see* p.100). The Jerusalem Film

Festival is held here in June. The big multiplexes are all based in the suburbs, screening the usual international films, largely in the original language.

Classical music

The city's main concert hall is the **Binyanei HaUma**, near the Central Bus Station. It is home to the Israel Philharmonic Orchestra, and is sometimes used by the Jerusalem Symphony Orchestra who are based at the **Henry Crown Symphony Hall**, Chopin Street (CU), which is the other main venue for classical concerts.

Classical events are some-times performed in other venues: the **Israel Museum** stages classical music most Tuesdays at 6pm, and **churches** are popular concert venues, such as the Church of the Dormition, on Mount Zion. Free concerts are often held at the **YMCA Auditorium**, King David Street, and the **Ticho House** (see p.102) hosts a Viennese salon each Saturday night, with a string quartet.

Other music venues

Classical concerts aside, there is a dearth of live music venues in Jerusalem. Try **Mike's**, on Horkenos Street, for nightly rock music; the **Tmol Shilshom** café-restaurant (see p.101) for folk and jazz; the **Ticho House** for jazz on Tuesday; and **Glasnost**, in the Russian Compound, for various styles. The main pop and rock venue is the **Yellow Submarine**, well out in the suburbs at Talpiot. Major rock (and classical) concerts are occasionally held in the **Sultan's Pool** amphi-theatre, which enjoys a marvellous atmospheric site in a depression just below the western City Wall.

A particularly nice venue which stages occasional concerts, of various kinds, is the **Khan**, an early-19C caravanserai, just off King David Street.

Sound-and-light shows

There are two son et lumière performances you might like to check out. The story of Jerusalem is told in sound and light in the courtyard of the **Citadel** (King David's Tower) every Monday, Wednesday and Saturday evening, translated into various languages. In addition, there is a biblical-themed murder-mystery-whodunnit every Saturday night at 10pm (☎ 02 626 5333 for details).

Out of the city, there is no more dramatic theatrical setting in the whole country than atop **Masada** (see p. 89).

Using state-of-the-art equipment and pyrotechnic effects, the history and heroic story of the Siege of Masada is played each Tuesday and Thursday in the summer (March-August 9pm, September-October 7pm). The show lasts 50 minutes and is presented in Hebrew, with simultaneous translations into various languages (reservations ☎ **07 995 9333**, Fax 07 995 5052).

SHOPPING

Jerusalem is not a city noted for its shopping, with comparatively few quality outlets and merchandise that is expensive compared to the West. Having said that, there are some intriguing purchases to be made, not least in the Old City where you can buy the whole gamut of war and peace, from a crown of thorns to a tee-shirt with the hawkish machine-gun slogan 'Uzi Does It'.

You can also compare the extreme experiences of shopping in one of the modern Western-style shopping malls with the noisy, vibrant, colourful bargaining of the bustling souqs.

Haggling

Haggling is the norm in much of Jerusalem, not just in the

Embroidered shirts.

souqs of the Old City. Many of the more old-fashioned shops in West Jerusalem do not display prices. Always try to get the buyer to state their price first. Go in beneath it (there is no magic percentage to aim for) and try to work out a price that you are both happy with. It's highly likely that the seller will be more expert than you at this process, but remember that you can always walk away and go elsewhere. If you are not sure whether you really want the item, don't haggle in the first place – it's considered very rude to bargain for your own amusement.

The Old City

The **souqs** of the Old City are as much a sightseeing attraction as a shopping opportunity. The first shops that most visitors come to, and therefore the most touristy, are along David Street. Here you can buy all the usual clichés of the Middle East: hookah or **hubble-bubble pipes** (*nargila*), **olive-wood carvings**, **fezes** and *keffiyas* (the Palestinian scarf made famous by Yasser Arafat), **leather sandals** (and lots of other leather goods), **copper and brassware** items (particularly coffee pots and trays) and, of course, **carpets**. If you don't want to haggle, try David Street's **Bazaar Shopping Centre**, where all the prices are fixed and there is no pushy salesman calling out, 'Hey, you like Manchester United?' Go further inside the warren and you will find the **Central Souqs**, the most colourful of all the Old City's shops, selling mostly clothes (*see* p.52).

Good cheap buys in the Old City include: Middle Eastern **sweetmeats**, though if you buy them loose from an itinerant trader, bargain hard; ubiquitous olive-wood carvings, often inlaid with mother-of-pearl; and **Arabic cassettes**, though avoid obviously pirate copies which are probably of poor quality.

The place for **religious goods** is, predictably, on and around the Via Dolorosa (*see* p.43).

A selection of water pipes for sale in the Christian Quarter.

Besides the bibles, rosary beads, crucifixes, icons and more serious items, there is enough kitsch to fill a 1950s museum: dimpled pink baby Jesus dolls, crowns of thorns, plastic Nativities with flashing lights and similar articles of dubious taste.

Other local specialities

Armenian ceramics make a beautiful souvenir. The obvious places to go are the two specialist ceramic shops on the Armenian Patriarchate Road, in the Armenian Quarter, though you will find it on sale elsewhere. One such place is Palestinian Pottery on the Nablus Road, en route to the American Colony (*see* p.54).

Dead Sea cosmetics (bath salts, mudpacks etc) which are sold worldwide, can be bought cheaper at source (*see* p.84) and are on sale all over Jerusalem.

The New City

Serious shoppers may like to browse the modern **malls** at the top of Ben Yehuda Street where it meets King George V Street (CU). However, there is little here that can't be bought more cheaply at home. Some of the shops directly below here, in the pedestrianised area known as the Midrahov, are well worth a visit, particularly those on Yoel Salomon Street. Many are devoted to **arts and crafts**, and feature beautiful ceramics, paintings, sculptures and jewellery. In the latter category, look for delicate filigreed **Yemenite jewellery** or **Roman glass** pieces, made with real blue opaque glass-shards from Roman times. Many items are hand-made and almost everything is expensive. This part of town is largely a haggle-free zone.

There is a **'hippy market'** at the bottom of Rivlin Street, open evenings (around 5 to 11pm) Sunday to Thursday, and on Friday morning. Keeping in tune with the street, it sells some nice craft items and clothes.

Armenian pottery store.

Judaica

Judaica refers to Jewish religious and ritual items and is the mainstay of many shops in West Jerusalem. Their window displays are typically old-fashioned and crammed with polished silverware, the favoured material for most pieces of Judaica. The best-known item is the *menora*, the seven-branched candelabra that is the national symbol (there is also a nine-branched version, used at Hanukkah). Also commonly fashioned in silver are Passover plates, wine goblets, Sabbath candlesticks and Havdala sets (used in a ritual to mark the end of the Sabbath).

Another popular item, often made in ceramic, is a *mezuza* (plural, *mezuzot*). This is a narrow, semicircular flattened tube, usually around 7.5-10cm (3-4in) long, in which is inserted a piece of paper or parchment inscribed with a passage from the Torah (the first five books of the Old Testament). *Mezuzot* are traditionally fastened beside the entrance door (look for them in the Jewish Quarter), always on the right-hand side, and next to the doors of the other rooms in the house, except the bathroom and toilet.

These days you don't have to settle for Judaica items just in silver. Israel has a thriving

modern art scene and this is sometimes married to pieces of Judaica with startling effects.

If you are serious about buying traditional Judaica, take a trip to the Ultra-Orthodox area of **Me'a She'arim** (see p.70) – though

you won't see any modern art frippery here. The **Cardo**★, in the Jewish Quarter (see p.42) is another good place, albeit expensive.

Judaica display in a shop on Ben Yehuda Street.

THE BASICS

Before You Go

Visitors entering Israel should have a full passport with at least six months left to run. Visitors' visas are issued free of charge to citizens from EU countries, Republic of Ireland, USA, Canada, Australia and New Zealand and are valid for up to three months. Be prepared for lots of questions with regard to security, and consequently a long check-in procedure. Beware too that if you have a stamp in your passport from any Arab countries that this can cause difficulties. If this is the case, then the best course of action is to apply for a visa, though this may take a few weeks to process. Conversely, an Israeli stamp in your passport can cause future problems if you intend travelling to Arab states. You should therefore request that only your visitor's visa, and not your passport, is stamped. No vaccinations are necessary.

Getting There

By Air: Ben-Gurion is Israel's main international airport, some 50km (31 miles) west of Jerusalem (in the south, Ovda, north of Eilat, handles charter flights). For airport information ☎ 03 971 0000, and for English-language flight information ☎ 03 971 2484. There are several direct scheduled flights to Israel from all over Europe (particularly the UK), the USA and Canada. The flight time from the UK to Tel Aviv is 4 hours 30 minutes. Many international airlines operate flights to Ben-Gurion, but the national carrier is **El Al** ☎ 020 7957 4100 for flight information in the UK, and in Jerusalem ☎ 02 624 5725.

By Ferry: If you have plenty of time, there is a ferry from Piraeus (Athens) to Haifa via Rhodes or Crete and Limassol, Cyprus. Call **Viamare Travel Ltd** ☎ 020 7431 4560 for information in the UK.

By Car: If you intend driving overland, note that only Egypt and Jordan have open land borders with Israel.

Arriving

There is a lengthy check-in procedure on arrival at the airport, and even more questions are asked on departure. Visitors should allow plenty of time for this (at least two hours before the departure time of your flight). Non-Israeli travellers must complete an embarkation card before passing passport control.

From Ben-Gurion airport **Egged** run a frequent bus service (around every 40 minutes, operating from around 6.30am-9.40pm) to the Central Bus Station, in West Jerusalem, which takes about 45 minutes and costs around 17-20NIS.

If you want door-to-door service, take a *sherut* (shared service taxi). Usually small mini-buses, the *sheruts* operate 24 hours, leaving when full, and will drop you at your hotel or a private address in Jerusalem. Run by the Nesher Taxi company (21 King George V Street), the trip costs around 40-45NIS, at least half the price of private or 'special' taxis, which are notorious for over-charging. You can book a *sherut* for your return to the airport on ☎ **02 623 1231/625 7227/625 5332**. Official fares are posted on a large sign in the arrivals hall, but agree this before you get into a private cab.

The Dome of the Rock.

A-Z

Accidents and Breakdowns

Contact the rental firm in the event of an accident or breakdown. In the event of an accident, exchange names, addresses and insurance details, but on no account move the vehicle, even if you are causing a hold-up, as this may affect your insurance claim. To contact the police ☎ 100, ambulance ☎ 911.
See also **Driving, Emergencies**

Accommodation *see* p.93

Airports *see* **Getting There** p.110

Banks

Most banks are open 8.30am-noon and 4-5.30/6pm Sunday, Tuesday and Thursday. On Monday, Wednesday and Friday they do not re-open in the afternoon. They are closed all day Saturday and national holidays. Many major banks have a money-changing desk open in the afternoons. The airport bureau de change is open 24 hours, though the rates are not good. Cash can also be changed at the Tourist Office near Jaffa Gate.

A passport is required if you are changing money. Travellers' cheques are widely accepted, but can attract a hefty minimum commission in banks, so always ask first. You can find automated teller machines (ATMs) in the New City, and traditional money-changers in East Jerusalem and the Arab part of the Old City (note that the moneychangers often offer the best rates, usually without commission charges for cash or travellers' cheques). Cash can be changed at most hotels, although the exchange rate may not be very favourable. The main international credit cards are widely accepted.
See also **Money**

Breakdowns *see* **Accidents**

Car Hire

There are numerous international and local car-hire agencies (the best known of which is **Eldan**) at the airport and in the New City. Local companies offer the best rates, but check that insurance and unlimited mileage are included in the price quoted. By the time you have added on insurance, rates can be very expensive compared to those in Europe, and given the difficulty of driving and parking in Jerusalem it is probably not worth the effort of hiring a car unless you intend seeing the rest of the country. While a car will give you the flexibility to travel further afield, short excursions are well catered for by public transport and tour operators (*see* **Tours**). Accidents are frequent, so you are strongly advised to take out fully comprehensive cover.

You must be at least 21 to hire a car and some hire companies specify that drivers must be over 24.

Most car hire companies have their main offices on King David Street, so you can shop around for the best deals. Many also have offices at the airport.
Avis 22 King David Street ☎ **02 624 9001**
Budget 23 King David Street ☎ **02 625 8986**
Eldan 24 King David Street

☎ **02 625 2151/2152/2153**
Europcar & Eurodollar 8 King David Street ☎ **02 623 5467**
Hertz 18 King David Street ☎ **02 623 1351**
See also **Driving, Accidents and Breakdowns**

Churches see **Religion**

Climate see **p.91**

Clothing

Late spring and all of autumn are warm and pleasant times of the year to visit Jerusalem; light clothes can be worn during the day, with an extra sweater or jacket for the evenings and cooler days. The summer months can be quite hot and a hat is essential for protection

Palestinian schoolgirls.

against the sun (especially if a trip to the Dead Sea and Masada is planned). Winters are cold and wet, so take some warm clothing and rain protection.

Casual wear is very much the norm, although smarter clothing will not be out of place in the dining rooms of 5-star hotels and smarter restaurants. When visiting churches and other holy places, remember that bare legs and arms are not acceptable and may well be forbidden.

Clothing sizes in Israel are the same as in Europe.

Women's sizes

UK	8	10	12	14	16	18
Europe	38	40	42	44	46	48
US	6	8	10	12	14	16

Women's shoes

UK	4.5	5	5.5	6	6.5	7
Europe	38	38	39	39	40	41
US	6	6.5	7	7.5	8	8.5

Men's suits

UK/US	36	38	40	42	44	46
Europe	46	48	50	52	54	56

Men's shirts

UK/US	14	14.5	15	15.5	16	16.5	17
Europe	36	37	38	39/40	41	42	43

Men's shoes

UK	7	7.5	8.5	9.5	10.5	11
Europe	41	42	43	44	45	46
US	8	8.5	9.5	10.5	11.5	12

Consulates and Embassies

As the status of Jerusalem as the capital of Israel is not internationally accepted, most embassies are in Tel Aviv, while the consulates are based in Jerusalem, usually with one in East Jerusalem (for Palestine) and one in West Jerusalem (for Israel).

Embassies

Australia: 37 Shaul HaMelekh Avenue, Tel Aviv ☎ 03 695 0451

Canada: 3 Nirim Street, Tel Aviv ☎ 03 636 3300

Ireland: 266 HaYarkon Street, Tel Aviv ☎ 03 950 9055

USA: 71 HaYarkon Street, Tel Aviv ☎ 03 519 7575

Consulates

British: Tower House, HaRakkevet Street, West Jerusalem ☎ 02 582 8281 19 Nashashibi Street, Sheikh Jarrah, PO Box 19690, East Jerusalem ☎ 02 582 8263

USA: 16 Agron Street, West Jerusalem ☎ 02 625 3288 27 Nablus Road, East Jerusalem ☎ 02 628 2231

Crime

Crime against tourists is not common in Jerusalem. None the less, it is advisable to take sensible precautions and be on your guard at all times, particularly in crowded parts of the Old City where pickpockets work. Beware that tourists have recently been assaulted on the

Ramparts Walk and on the Mount of Olives, and women should avoid these areas unless accompanied by males. Be on your guard at all times, and remember the following guidelines:

• Carry as little money and as few credit cards as possible, and leave any valuables in the hotel safe.

• Carry wallets and purses in secure pockets inside your outer clothing, and carry handbags across your body or firmly under your arm.

• If your passport is lost or stolen, report it to your holiday representative, Consulate or Embassy at once.

Currency see Money

Customs and Entry Regulations

The duty-free allowance for adults (aged over 17 years) is: up to 250g of tobacco products or 250 cigarettes; 1 litre of spirits and 2 litres of wine; 250cl of perfume; and $200 worth of gifts.

Disabled Visitors

Although the Old City of Jerusalem is not an easy place for wheelchairs, elsewhere facilities are relatively good. This is due in no small part to the large number of service personnel disabled in the country's recent numerous conflicts.

In Britain, contact **Holiday Care Service**, 2nd Floor, Imperial Buildings, Victoria Road, Horley, Surrey RH6 7PZ ☎ **01293 774 535**, www.free-space.virgin.net/hol.care. They can supply details on accommodation, transport and tour operators.

RADAR also publishes holiday information for disabled travellers. Contact them at 12 City Forum, 250 City Road, London EC1V 8AF ☎ **020 7250 3222**; www.radar. org.uk. An informative 12-page information sheet *Wheelchair Accessible Travel in Israel* is available both from the Israeli Government Tourist Office in London (*see* p.123) and on line at www.yadsarah.org.il/ Tourists/Wheelchair.html. See also the associated web site www.yadsarah.org.il/Tourists/ friendly_tour.html. Wheelchairs and other aids are loaned free of charge (deposit payable) by the Yad Sarah organisation, 43 Hanevi'im Street ☎ **02 644 4444**.

The best guide book is *Access in Israel*, available in the UK from Access Project, 39 Bradley Gardens, West Ealing, London W13 8HE, e-mail: gordon. couch@virgin.net.

Driving

The standard of driving in Israel is poor, averaging over 10 deaths per day in a country the size of Wales. Remember to drive on the RIGHT, and to give way to traffic coming from the left. Street parking in Jerusalem is nearly always difficult. Never leave valuables in the car, as theft is common.

There are no motorways but road surfaces are usually good. Signposting is in Hebrew and English, but can be confusing.

The following speed limits apply:

Country roads 90kph/56mph
Built-up areas 50kph/31mph

Drivers need carry only a full national driving licence. The wearing of seatbelts is compulsory.

Note that most car hire companies stipulate that you should not take their car (which bears Israeli number plates) into the Palestinian territories. *See also* **Accidents and Breakdowns**

Electric Current

The voltage in Israel is usually 220V. Plugs and sockets are of the round-fitting three-pin Continental European variety. Travellers from elsewhere should bring an adaptor. North American appliances may also need a transformer.

Embassies *see* Consulates

Emergencies

Police ☎ **100**
Ambulance ☎ **101** (Hebrew speaking)
or ☎ **911** (English speaking)
Fire ☎ **102**

Etiquette

As Israel is probably the world's most disputed land, and Jerusalem its most disputed city, it is best to steer clear of discussing politics.

When visiting major churches and holy places visitors should always be wary of offending, however innocently, the multiplicity of religious sensibilities, that may be in play. For example, in the Church of the Holy Sepulchre the priests may well hiss at you if you sit down and cross your legs! As a starting point, dress discreetly (no shorts, vests or revealing tops) then watch what other visitors are doing. It's always best to keep a low profile. Surprisingly, photography is usually permitted inside churches, though not in the Dome of the Rock. Also refrain from taking pictures of the Western Wall on the Sabbath.

In service situations Israelis can be brusque.

Guidebooks *see* Maps

Health

The quality of healthcare in Israel is generally high, but visitors are charged for all services, so make sure you are fully insured. Lists of doctors can be obtained from hotels, chemists or by looking in the *Jerusalem Post*. Tourists can call the special medical helpline on ☎ 177 022 9110.

Hours see Opening Hours

Information see Tourist Information Offices

Language

The official state languages are Hebrew and Arabic, though English is a compulsory school subject and French is also widely spoken. The majority of Jersualemites, particularly in the West, speak excellent English. In East Jerusalem Arabic is the lingua franca, though here too you will generally be understood. It is difficult for the visitor to master either Hebrew or Arabic but any efforts to speak even a few simple words and expressions are often warmly received, particularly by the Arabs. Below are a few words and phrases to attempt.

Maps

The free *Jerusalem City Map*, compliments of H Stern (the jewellers), is a reasonable starting point. If your hotel does not have a copy, pick one up at their shop inside the Jaffa Gate. For a more detailed

English	Hebrew	Arabic
Yes	ken	ay-wah
No	lo	la
Please	bekava-sha	min fadlach
Thank you	to-dah	shoo-kran
Good morning	boker tov	sabah al-kheir
Good evening	erev tov	masa al-kheir
Hello/Goodbye	shalom	salaam
How much (is this)?	ka-mah?	ah-desh hadah?
Where is ...?	aye-fo ...?	feen ...?
I don't understand	Ani Lo mevin/mevina	mish faahim
Do you speak English?	Ata me-dah-behr angleet	tech-kee Ingleesi?

map, particularly of the Old City, look in any good bookshop. Those produced by MAP and Carta are recommended. The Tourist Office also supplies a free Jerusalem Visitors' Map which is quite adequate.

Note that sometimes the names of streets are written differently on maps and on street signs. For example:

on map	on street sign
Ha-Melekh George V	King George V Street
Ben Hillel	Hillel Street
Yafo	Jaffa Street
Shelomzion Ha-Malka	Queen Shlomzion
Josef Rivlin	Joseph Rivlin Street
Bāb es Silsila	Bab El-Silsileh Road

Money

The monetary unit of Israel is the *shekel* or, as it is now known, the New Israeli Shekel (NIS). There are 100 *agorot* to the *shekel*. Notes are issued in denominations of NIS 200, 100, 50, 20 and 10. Coins are NIS 1, 5, 10 and 50; and 10 and 5 *agorot*. All major credit cards (American Express, Carte Bleue [Visa/Barclaycard], Eurocard [Mastercard/Access] and Diners Club) are accepted in most shops, restaurants and hotels. You will see many prices (and all hotel rooms) quoted in US dollars, which are widely accepted as cash. In fact, it is actually best to pay for hotel bills, car hire and organised tours in foreign currency as this means you are exempt from the 17% VAT.

There are no restrictions on the amount of foreign currency visitors can take into Israel. As travellers' cheques are so expensive to cash, plastic is probably the best bet. Bureaux de change desks are found at the airport and banks. Exchange rates vary, so it pays to shop around. *See also* **Banks**

Newspapers

Most British and foreign newspapers and magazines can be bought in Jerusalem. The English-language *Jerusalem Post* carries world, European and British news, even down to football results (daily, except Saturdays). The Friday edition is particularly useful for its listings supplement. The *Jerusalem Post* may be rather right-wing for some. More liberal in tone is the national daily *Ha'aretz*, which is published in English and Hebrew. Also in English is the Palestinian paper, the weekly *Jerusalem Times*, which covers Palestinian news only.

Visitors will probably come across copies of the free monthly *Traveller* in bars and hostels, which has useful tips on where to go and where to eat cheaply. The monthly *Your Jerusalem* (free, from Safra Square tourist office) also contains useful listings.

Opening Hours

Visitors who wish to make the most of their stay, and visit as many places as possible, should start early in the morning and organise their itinerary very carefully as most sites close early in the afternoon, others open only on certain days and times of the week and, to make matters more confusing still, the day of rest is different in the Arab, Jewish and Christian quarters. In general, West Jerusalem comes to a halt on the Sabbath (*shabbat*), which runs from sundown on Friday night to sundown on Saturday night. East Jerusalem's Muslim day of rest is Friday.

Shops: Traditional shop opening hours are 8/9am-1pm and 4pm-7pm Sunday to Thursday, Friday 8/9am-2pm. Tourist shops may remain open throughout the day. Christian shops close on Sunday.

Chemists: These are generally open traditional shop hours, and lists of those which are open emergency hours can be found in the *Jerusalem Post*.

Museums: Generally open 9/10am-5pm Sunday to Thursday; some also open 9/10am-2pm Friday and Saturday 10am-2pm.

Churches: Times vary but many are closed for an hour or two in the middle of the day. *See also* **Banks, Post Offices**

Photography

Good-quality film and camera equipment are readily available, but at prices well above those in Europe, so you should stock up on films before you go. Photography is often restricted in museums, though (surprisingly) not in many churches. Beware if taking pictures of people, however – some Orthodox Jews and Arabs

resent this (*see* **Etiquette**).
Never leave your cameras in a
car.

Police

There is a tourist police service
in Jerusalem, though they
generally keep a low profile.
Armed soldiers guard potential
religious flashpoints, and are a
common sight throughout the
city. In an emergency ☎ **100**.

Post Offices

General opening hours are
8am-12 noon and 3.30-6.30pm
Sunday to Thursday, 8am-1pm
Wednesday, 8am-noon Friday.
They provide all the usual
postal facilities and larger ones

Greek Orthodox priest.

will also exchange money. The
main West Jerusalem office is
on the Jaffa Road, open 7am-
7pm Sunday-Thursday, and
Friday until noon, and is where
poste restante mail is delivered
to. You can often buy stamps
together with postcards, or
from your hotel.

Public Holidays

With so many faiths and different calendar interpretations
there is a public holiday of one
kind or another most days in
Jerusalem. To complicate
matters, both Jewish and
Islamic holidays follow lunar
calendars, rather than the
Gregorian (Western) calendar,
which is also adhered to in
daily life. The lunar calendar is
shorter, so to get back in line
with the Gregorian system, the
Jewish calendar adds a month
every few years. The Muslim
calendar does not and so falls
behind each year by around 11
days. This means that religious
holidays fall on different days
each year. The different Christian denominations complicate
the picture further, following
either the Gregorian calendar
or the Julian calendar.

The following are the main
Jewish holy days, when most
shops and public services,
including transport, close
down:

Purim Feb/March
Passover March/April
Pentecost May/June
Rosh Hashana (New Year)
  September/October
Yom Kippur (Day of Atonement)
  September/October
Sukkot September/October
Simhat Torah week after Sukkot
  There are Israeli public
holidays on:
Holocaust Day April/May
Independence Day April/May
  Other Jewish festivals which
do not involve closures are
Hanukkah (Nov/Dec); *Purim*
(Feb/March); *Tu Bishvat*
(Jan/Feb).
  Islamic festivals tend to be
less disruptive than Jewish
ones. Following the lunar
calendar, they fall on different
dates each year. The main ones
are (*denotes public holiday):
*Eid al-Adha** Feb/March
Al-Hijra (New Year)
  March/April
Moulid al-Nabi May/June
Ramadan (beginning) Nov
*Eid al-Fitr** (end of Ramadan)
  Dec/Jan
  In addition, on 15 May all
Arab shops, cafés and restau-
rants close to commemorate
the *Naqba* (The Great
Disaster), when the Palestini-
ans lost their land with the
creation of the State of Israel.
  Christian festivals vary, with
Western denominations

celebrating Christmas, for
example, on 25 December
while the Orthodox church
celebrates it on 7 January and
the Armenian on 19 January.
Similarly, the Eastern church
celebrations for Easter follow a
couple of weeks after the
Roman Catholic and Protestant dates.
  The **Armenian Quarter** shuts
down on 24 April to commemorate the Armenian genocide
in 1915.

Religion
Jerusalem is home to churches
of every different denomina-
tion and nationality, all of
whom worship freely in their
own right. For details of
services, ask at the main tourist
office, your hotel, or look in
the *Jerusalem Post*.

Smoking
Smoking is banned in most
public places, although this
regulation is widely flouted.

Taxis *see* **Transport**

Telephones
You can dial anywhere in Israel
and abroad from street
telephone kiosks. These take
phonecards, purchased from
newsagents, kiosks, vending
machines and post offices. At
the time of writing, the most

useful networks for making calls overseas were:

Bezeq, cheapest to the US and Ireland (access code ☎ 001); and **Barak**, cheapest to UK, Canada, Australia and New Zealand (access code ☎ 013). For calls to France, Bezeq and Barak cost the same. However prices change, so compare these two and also **Golden Lines** (access code ☎ 012), if possible. For an international call, dial the carrier's access code (e.g. 001 for Bezeq), then the country code without the 00, (44 for the UK), the city code and the subscriber number.

There is a small but growing number of Internet bars and cafés in the New City, such as Strudel, Monbaz Street; Tmol Shilshom, Yoel Salomon Street (*see* p.101); and Netcafé, Heleni Ha-Malka Street. Calls and faxes can also be made from the **International Phone Centre** at Koresh Street (236 Jaffa Road), open Sunday to Thursday 8am until late, or at **Solan Communications**, on A M Lunz Street (off King George V Street), which is open 24 hours. You can also fax from main post offices.

Telephone calls made from hotels are very expensive. Cheap rates apply 1-8am. For local directory enquiries

☎ 144
For international operator
☎ 188
For international directory enquiries ☎ 188
Country codes are as follows:
Australia ☎ 00 61
Canada ☎ 00 1
Ireland ☎ 00 353
New Zealand ☎ 00 64
UK ☎ 00 44
USA ☎ 00 1
To call Israel from abroad ☎ 00 972. The area code for Jerusalem is 02 (omit the zero if dialling from abroad). The area code for Tel Aviv is ☎ 03.

Time Difference

Israel is on GMT+2hrs all year, and is seven hours ahead of American Eastern Standard Time.

Tipping

In recent years Israel has become very tip conscious. Service workers are generally poorly paid and rely on tips to supplement their pay. If a service charge (usually 15%) is not already included in the restaurant bill, then the waiter or waitress will write on the bill (in large letters, often with a smiley face) 'service not included'. It is customary to tip hotel-room maids around 6NIS per night. Taxi drivers, surprisingly, don't expect a tip.

Tourist Information Offices

The **Israel Government Tourist Office (IGTO)** is a good initial source of information, including accommodation, travel and places of interest. Check out their web site: www.infotour. co.il. It has offices in the following countries:

Australia: Australia-Israel Chamber of Commerce Tourism Dept, 395 New South Head Road, Double Bay, Sydney, NSW 2028 ☎ (02) 9326 1700

Canada: Israel Government Tourist Office, 180 Bloor Street West, Suite 700, Toronto, Ontario M5S 2V6 ☎ 800 669 2369, (416) 964 3784

UK: Israel Government Tourist Office, UK House, 180 Oxford Street, London W1N 9DJ ☎ (020) 7299 1111

USA: Israel Government Tourist Office, 800 Second Avenue, New York, NY 10017 ☎ (212) 499 5650.

Tourist offices in Jerusalem

The main tourist information centre in Jerusalem is in the City Hall complex, on Safra Square ☎ 02 625 8844, Fax 02 624 9430 (open 9am-4.30pm Sunday to Thursday, 9am-noon Friday). There is another tourist information office just inside the Jaffa Gate (Omar Ibn al-Khattab Square), ☎ 02 628 0382, Fax 02 628 0457, which is run by Solan Communications (open 9am-7pm Sunday to Thursday, 9am-4pm Friday). Further round on Omar Ibn al-Khattab Square is the Christian Information Centre ☎ 02 627 2692, Fax 02 628 6417, which is very useful for information on East Jerusalem, Christian sites and hostel accommodation (open 8.30am-1pm Monday to Saturday).

Tours

The tour operator **Egged** offers a round-tour of the city by bus **no 99**, which takes around 90

minutes and provides a good introduction to Jerusalem and is really worth doing. Among the 27 stops, which include the Israel Museum, Bible Lands Museum, Yad VaShem and the Knesset, don't miss the Haas Promenade (stop no 6) which offers extensive views of the Old City and will help you understand the whole layout of Jerusalem. If you are interested in diamonds, stop no 7 takes you to the National Diamond Centre on Hebron Road (Derekh Hevron). Stop no 10, Holyland Hotel, is also worth a visit to the gardens for the large plan of Jerusalem (scale 1/50, *see* p.31) as it was in the time of the Second Temple (the Holyland Hotel can also be reached by taking bus no 21 from Zion/Ziyyon Square). It is a hop-on, hop-off service, though beware that at peak times buses are so full it may not be possible to hop back on! Also make sure you get on a bus with a guide who speaks your language if possible; enquiries and tickets from the Jaffa Gate tourist office (the tour starts at the Jaffa Gate).

There are numerous **coach tours** to Bethlehem; to the Dead Sea, including Masada and Ein Gedi (*see* p.86 for an alternative tour); to Galilee and Nazareth etc. Pick up details from tourist offices, travel agents, **Egged ☎ 02 530 4704/629 6041**, or visit the Egged web site www.egged. co.il.

You need to walk to explore the Old City. The city council run a free tour every Saturday at 10am, departing from the City Hall complex, 32 Jaffa Road, lasting around 3 hours. Another free tour departs from the Sheraton Plaza Hotel (open to non-residents) most days at 9am. There are various fee-paying walking city tours, each with its own slant. **Zion Walking Tours ☎ 02 628 7866**, based opposite the Citadel, have a good reputation. Pick up a flyer from the tourist office. **Archaeological Walking Tours**, 34 Habad ☎ **02 627 1333**, offer 3-hour tours of Jewish archaeological sites, and an underground walk in the controversial Western Wall tunnel (prior booking essential).

For a bird's-eye view of Jerusalem and the surrounding area, book a half-hour **air tour** with **Jerusalem Wings** (☎ **02 583 1444**). It costs around $50. They also fly to Masada and back (non-stop) for around $90.

For a personal guided tour, book the services of the lively and knowledgeable Moshe

Mor, a Jerusalem resident who is also expert on most other aspects of the country. He is fully licensed and gives tours in impeccable English or French ☎ 02 563 9699; cellphone 052 408561.

Transport

You can see most of the Old City and the New City on foot.
Buses: The generally efficient bus service is run by **Egged** ☎ 02 530 4704, though services are less frequent in East Jerusalem (a couple of independent Palestinian operators serve the area east of the Green line). The main Egged bus station is west of Zion Square, on Jaffa Road. Buses run from around 5.30am until around midnight, and there is a single fare within the city limits. Tickets are bought from the driver. Note that on Fridays or on the eve of Jewish holidays Egged buses stop at 3 or 4pm until sunset on Saturday.

The Palestinian buses operate from the stations on Nablus Road (Derekh Shekhem) and Sultān Suleimān Road. These buses are more variable in quality, with a definite trend to the bottom of the scale for comfort.

A glass sculpture exhibition, held in the Citadel grounds.

There are numerous public buses to Yad VaShem, including nos 13, 17, 20 and 23. Bus nos 17 (which also goes to the Israeli Museum), 18 and 20 run along King George V Street and the Jaffa Road. To get to the Mount of Olives, take bus no 37 or 75 (Palestine bus) from the Damascus Gate.

Taxis: Taxis can be hailed in the street or your hotel will call one for you (though this is no guarantee of quality). They are often expensive and many overcharge. In order to prevent tourists from being taken advantage of, fares from the airport are now prominently displayed, and some of the larger hotels are doing likewise, listing fares to the more popular places. You must, however, still make sure you agree the fare before stepping into the cab (the meter is usually 'broken').

TV and Radio

Israel has two state-run TV channels, both featuring English-language programmes. Channel 1 has the news in English at 6.15pm from Monday to Thursday, at 4.30pm on Friday, at 5pm on Saturday. It is likely that your hotel will also have a choice of cable and satellite channels.

Radio West (102.8 FM) is an English-language talk station, with news on the hour. BBC World Service can be picked up on the medium wave at 1322 kHz (if not try 227, 639 or 1413 Khz). See the *Jerusalem Post* for more detailed listings.

Vaccinations see Before You Go p.110

Water

Tap water is safe to drink, though bottled water is the popular alternative.

INDEX